CHRISTMAS COOKBOOK

Mouthwatering, Delicious, Simple Christmas Crock Pot Recipes

(Homemade Delicious Christmas Feasts to Make Your Family)

Amanda Obryan

Published by Alex Howard

© **Amanda Obryan**

All Rights Reserved

Christmas Cookbook: Mouthwatering, Delicious, Simple Christmas Crock Pot Recipes (Homemade Delicious Christmas Feasts to Make Your Family)

ISBN 978-1-990169-47-2

All rights reserved. No part of this guide may be reproduced in any form without permission in writing from the publisher except in the case of brief quotations embodied in critical articles or reviews.

Legal & Disclaimer

The information contained in this book is not designed to replace or take the place of any form of medicine or professional medical advice. The information in this book has been provided for educational and entertainment purposes only.

The information contained in this book has been compiled from sources deemed reliable, and it is accurate to the best of the Author's knowledge; however, the Author cannot guarantee its accuracy and validity and cannot be held liable for any errors or omissions. Changes are periodically made to this book. You must consult your doctor or get professional medical advice before using any of the suggested remedies, techniques, or information in this book.

Table of contents

PART 1 1
1. DO YOU DREAD PLANNING YOUR CHRISTMAS FEAST? 2
2. THE FOIL WRAPPED ROASTING METHOD REVEALED 4
3. TURKEY STRING LIFT - HOW TO DO 6
4. APPETIZERS 7
   4.1. GREEK ARTICHOKE APPETIZER 7
   4.2. COUSCOUS-STUFFED MUSHROOMS 9
   4.3. DEVILED EGGS WITH BACON SRIRACHA AVOCADO FILLING 11
   4.4. UNCOMMONLY DELIGHTFUL PROVENÇAL DEVILED EGGS 12
   4.5. GREEN OLIVES AND ARTICHOKE HEARTS TAPENADE 13
   4.6. SPANAKOPITA BITES 14
   4.7. TITAINA 16
   4.8. TORTILLA ESPANOLA 17
   4.9. SPANISH PAN-FRIED SHRIMP WITH GARLIC 19
5. MAIN COURSE RECIPES 20
   5.1. STANDING BEEF RIB ROAST AND GRAVY 20
   5.2. ITALIAN STYLE CHICKEN WITH PEAS AND BACON 21
   5.3. PORTUGUESE CHRISTMAS LEG OF LAMB 23
   5.4. PORK ROAST AND GRAVY 24
   5.5. GREEK CHRISTMAS PORK ROAST 26
   5.6. SPICE RUBBED PORK LOIN ROAST 28
   5.7. HOW TO MAKE THE MOST DELICIOUS TURKEY EVER 29
   5.8. APPLE-SHALLOT ROASTED TURKEY 31
   5.9. ASIAN SPICED CHRISTMAS TURKEY 33
   5.10. FRIED TURKEY BREAST AND GRAVY 35
   5.11. GARLIC AND HERB ROASTED TURKEY 37
   5.12. GARLIC HERB BACON WRAPPED TURKEY BREAST 39
   5.13. GRILLED TUSCAN STYLE TURKEY 40
   5.14. INDIAN-SPICED TURKEY BREAST 41
   5.15. LEMON ROSEMARY BRINED TURKEY 43
   5.16. MOTHER MITCHELL'S TURKEY AND DRESSING 45

5.17. Turkey And Yam Shepherd's Pie 47

6. SIDE DISHES AND CONDIMENTS 49

6.1. Broiled Asparagus With Lemon-Shallot 49
6.2. Roasted Asparagus With Caper Dressing 50
6.3. Broccoli Bake 51
6.4. Broccoli And Beef Short Ribs 52
6.5. Chinese Style Broccoli 53
6.6. Roman Style Broccoli 54
6.7. Balsamic-Braised Bacon Brussels Sprouts 55
6.8. Bang Bang Brussels Sprouts 56
6.9. Roasted Brussels Sprouts With Garlic Aioli 57
6.10. Brussels Sprouts And Toasted Pecans 59
6.11. Easy Brown Sugar Glazed Carrots 60
6.12. Simple Glazed Carrots 61
6.13. Gingered Carrots 62
6.14. Garlicky Mashed Cauliflower 63
6.15. Sweetest Corn On The Cob 65
6.16. Cranberry Conserve 66
6.17. Classic Green Bean Casserole 67
6.18. Savory Green Beans With Caramelized Onions 68
6.19. Green Beans With Pine Nuts And Mozzarella 69
6.20. Italian-Style Green Beans 70
6.21. Easy Hot Potatoes 71
6.22. Mustard Mashed Potatoes 72
6.23. Savory Mashed Potatoes 73
6.24. Baked Yam Casserole 75
7. Special Desserts 76
7.1. Apple Frangipane Tart 76
7.2. Nectarine Almond Frangipane Tart 78
7.3. Orange Coconut Pecan Pie 81
7.4. Roasted Pears With Dark Chocolate Hazelnut Sauce 83
7.5. Pecan Pie Cobbler 84
7.6. Strawberry Surprise Cake 86
7.7 Very French Cherry Dessert 87
Bonus Recipe Section 88

Arroz Caldo	89
Divine Chicken Divan	91
Parisienne Chicken And Rice Bake	93
Garlic Seasoned Vegetables	94
Hungarian Goulash With Yellow Onions	95
Pork Estofado	96
Roasted Shiitakes And Pacific Cod	98

PART 2 99

INTRODUCTION 100

1. Beef Pot Roast With Turnip Greens	101
2. Cinnamon Roll Casserole	103
3. Slow Cooker Glazed Ham	104
4. Sweet And Spicy Cranberry Meatballs	105
5. Slow-Cooker Falling-Off-The-Bone Short Ribs	107
6. Slow-Cooker Triple Chocolate Brownies	109
7. Christmas Slow Cooker Whole Chicken	110
8. Ham Steaks And Pineapple Rings	111
9. Turkey Breast And Gravy	112
10. Nutella French Toast Casserole With Caramelized Bananas	113
11. Slow-Cooker Turtle Monkey Bread	114
12. Slow Cooker Christmas Cocoa	115
13. French Toast Casserole	116
14. Slow Cooker Christmas Pudding	117
15. Slow Cooker Candy Cane White Hot Chocolate	119
Raspberry Almonds Squares	120
Peanut Butter And Banana S'mores	122
Vegan Tiramisu	123
Pumpkin Ice Cream And Brownie Parfait	126
Pumpkin Mousse Tarts	128
Chocolate Hazelnut Cheesecake	130
Chocolate Pumpkin Tart	132
Mocha Ice Cream Sandwiches	134
Healthy Oreo Cake	138
Chocolate Kale Brownies	140
Mini Crunch Bars With Peanut Butter Shell Drizzle	141

- Raw Coconut Snowballs 143
- Raw Spice Cookie Dough Bites 144
- Spiced Cacao Raw Cookie Dough Bites... 145
- Deep Dish Cookie Pie 147
- Apricot & Salt Chocolate Tart.. 148
- Apricot Chocolate Filling 149
- Rocky Road Fudge 150
- Black Bean Apple Brownies 151
- Chocolate Pots De Crème 153
- Blueberry Lime Cheesecake 154
- Pumpkin Pie 156
- Blueberry, Lemon, Poppy Seed & Almond Cake 158
- Blueberry Crisp Tart With Oat Crust 160
- Summer Berry Crisps 162
- Dark Chocolate Cereal Cookies 163
- Chocolate Cereal Cookies 164
- Boomin Style Onion Rings.. 165
- Arugula And Cremini Quiche With Gluten-Free Almond Meal Crust 166
- Directions 166

GINGERBREAD DOUGH/HOUSE 168

- Candy.. 169
- Cashew Beef 170
- Ground Sirloin 172
- Sirloin Tip Chili 174
- Orange Beef Stew 176
- Vegetable Beef 178
- Dark Cherry Stew... 179
- Jalapeno Beef.. 180
- Spicy Shredded Beef Chuck 181
- Beef Chuck & Spices 182
- Beef Chili 184
- Oregano Beef Sirloin.. 186
- Spicy Beef Stew 187
- Garlic Beef Shoulder.. 188
- Ginger Beef 189

Part 1

1. Do You Dread Planning Your Christmas Feast?

Are you "young" enough to remember the 'Chinese Menu' method of ordering a meal?

Remember: "Pick 1 from Column A, two from Column B, and…."

Inside this book, you'll find a multitude of compatible dishes that you can combine with impunity to make fantastic, magical, and nutritious meals for your family and friends, effortlessly!

Every dish is scalable: you can feed large or small groups by merely increasing or decreasing the amounts of each ingredient!

No more are you bound to a rigid set of rules **(example: 'Serves 6')**!

Appetizers!

Here are wonderful appetizer dishes, each a delicacy in its own right. Mix, match, and combine to form exquisite and delectable arrays that are sure to please.

Main Dishes!

Select one or more from a dazzling display of magnificent main dishes. Know that each selection will complement the others. Your guests will be amazed at your culinary prowess!

Vegetables and Side Dishes!

Your meal plan will be replete with smart choices, no matter which of these side dishes you choose. No more fumbling for a suitable companion piece. Just choose away with abandon!

Desserts!

No meal should languish because of a dull desert. You can short-circuit that with any one of these taste-tempting comestibles. Each is easy to make, a delight to consume. I predict no leftovers here!

Your dining combinations are almost endless! The flavors superb!

Using the 'Chinese Menu' techniques, if you only pick one recipe from each category you have over twenty-five thousand (25,704, to be exact) meal plans instantly at your fingertips! Choose two menu items from each category, and the number of meal plans expands exponentially!

No more will you have to struggle to assemble a credible and compatible menu.

What are you waiting for?

2. The Foil Wrapped Roasting Method Revealed

Most of our recipes are based on the "Foil Wrapped Method" of preparing and roasting a Turkey.

Wrapping and cooking the entire turkey in aluminum foil requires an increased oven temperature to ensure a completely cooked turkey. Preheating the oven to 450°F actually steams the turkey in its own juices. It produces a moist bird with a light golden, non-crisp skin. The cooking time is reduced due to higher temperatures and the trapped steam inside the foil.

Single Foil Sheet Directions:

Aluminum foil comes in two convenient sizes. The most common is a sheet 12 inches wide. The larger size is 18 inches wide. We use the 18-inch wide for our turkey wrap.

Tear off two pieces of 18-inch wide heavy-duty aluminum foil that are 2 times longer than the turkey. Lay one sheet on a suitable working surface larger than the foil. Place this second sheet on top of the first, aligning the long edges. Make a fold of both sheets about ¼-inch wide the entire length of the long side. Fold over and additional ¼-inch to make a long seam. Be sure to tightly crease the foil with your finger or a smooth wooden spoon to seal the two sheets together. Fold that 1/4" seam in half, lengthwise to make a liquid-tight seam. Open the two sheets like butterfly wings. You now have a very large sheet of aluminum foil with a seam down the centerline.

Spray a vegetable cooking oil, such as PAM®, along the center seam, and about a hand's with on either side where the foil will touch the turkey.

To Use:

Place a Turkey String Lift along the centerline. Place the turkey lengthwise in the middle of the **Single Foil Sheet** on top of the String Lift, breast side up. Bring the foil sides up and crimp over the turkey. Fold the ends closed and bring ends up overlapping the turkey. (Optional before cooking) Insert a meat thermometer through the foil into the thickest part of the breast.

Place foil-wrapped turkey in a shallow roasting pan and place pan in a preheated 450°F. oven.

A 14 pound stuffed turkey will take less than 3 hours to be fully cooked by this method.

To brown turkey: open foil during last 20-30 minutes of cooking.

Roast until meat thermometer inserted in the innermost part of the thigh reads 165°F. Check the temperature in the thickest part of the breast and the wing as well. Temperature in all areas should be 165°F or higher.

Broth may accumulate in the foil during cooking. Reserve this flavorful broth for moistening stuffing or for making giblet gravy. Cooking time can be reduced by as much as 30 minutes to an hour compared to a traditional roasting timetable.

3. Turkey String Lift - How To Do

The most convenient method of moving a cooked turkey from its place in the wrapping foil to its place on the carving dish is through the use of a String Lift. While double carving forks can be used, the possibility of dropping the steaming hot bird are high.

The String Lift acts as a protective sling, surrounding the bird and making it easier to lift and to transport from cooking pan to carving dish.

Commercial String Lifts are available, however, it is our experience that most stores don't carry the Lifts because people are unfamiliar with them, don't know how to use them, and as a result commercial string lifts are not a great seller.

HOW TO MAKE A TURKEY STRING LIFT:
Cut an 80-inch length of heavy cotton Butcher's twine.
Knot ends together to make a loop. Put a single knot in center of loop.
Place second figure eight knot 3 inches to right of first knot.
Place third figure eight knot 3 inches to the left of first knot.
Center bird on center knot.
Draw string loops around and up over bird's wings and legs during cooking.

To Use:
Unwrap the foil from the turkey breast and the legs and wings.
Grasp a loop in each hand.
Gently lift the turkey straight up off of the foil sheet.
Ask a helper to loosen any foil that tries to cling to the turkey as it is being hoisted.
Move the turkey to the cutting board and drape the Sling Lift away from the turkey.
It is not necessary to remove the Lift from under the turkey while carving the bird.

4. Appetizers

Jump start your Christmas feast with selections from this dazzling array of World-famous recipes designed to tantalize and heighten your guests' dining experience!

4.1. Greek Artichoke Appetizer

Ingredients:
2–6 oz. jars marinated artichoke hearts, divided
1 small onion, finely chopped
1½ cloves garlic, minced
4 large eggs, beaten
¼ cup dry bread crumbs
¼ teaspoon salt
⅛ teaspoon ground black pepper
¼ teaspoon dried oregano
½ teaspoon hot pepper sauce (such as Tabasco®)
¾ pound sharp Cheddar cheese, shredded
2 tablespoons minced fresh parsley
1 teaspoon grated Parmesan cheese

Directions:
Preheat oven to 325°F.
Grease a 13x9-inch glass baking dish.
Drain marinade from one jar of artichoke hearts into a skillet.
Pour artichoke hearts from drained jar and the entire second jar (marinade and artichoke hearts) into a food processor.
Blend until artichoke hearts are coarsely chopped and set aside.
Cook and stir onion and garlic in the skillet with marinade over medium-low heat until onions are light brown, 5 to 7 minutes.
Remove from heat and transfer to a large bowl.

Stir onion mixture, eggs, bread crumbs, salt, black pepper, oregano, and hot pepper sauce together until well mixed.

Stir sharp Cheddar cheese, parsley, Parmesan cheese, and chopped artichoke heart mixture into the onion mixture.

Pour mixture into prepared baking dish.

Bake in preheated oven until top is golden, 25 to 30 minutes.

Cut into 1-inch squares and serve warm or cold.

4.2. Couscous-Stuffed Mushrooms

Ingredients:
18 medium fresh cremini mushrooms
3 green onions, chopped
2 garlic cloves, minced
1 tablespoon olive or canola oil
1 cup dry white wine or low-sodium chicken broth
2 tablespoons low-sodium soy sauce
Filling:
½ cup low-sodium chicken broth
¼ cup uncooked couscous
⅓ cup minced fresh parsley
2 tablespoons chopped fresh basil or 2 teaspoons dried basil
¼ cup grated Romano cheese
1 egg white, lightly beaten
2 tablespoons chopped walnuts, toasted
¼ teaspoon salt
⅛ teaspoon pepper

Directions:
Preheat oven to 350°F.
Remove and discard mushroom stems. Set caps aside.
In a large nonstick skillet, heat oil to shimmering.
Sauté onions until translucent, then add garlic and sauté for 30 seconds.
Stir in wine or broth, soy sauce, and mushroom caps.
Bring to a boil.
Reduce heat, cover and simmer until mushrooms are tender.
Remove mushrooms with a slotted spoon, reserving liquid in skillet.
Place mushrooms stem side down on paper towels.
In another saucepan, bring broth to a boil.
Stir in couscous and mix to thoroughly submerge.

Remove saucepan from the heat, cover, and let stand for 5 minutes.
Fluff couscous with a fork and add to reserved mushroom liquid. Cover and cook on low heat until liquid is absorbed, about 5 minutes.
Add the next five ingredients (parsley through walnuts) and toss gently.
Sprinkle inside of mushroom caps with salt and pepper.
Stuff with couscous mixture.
Arrange in an 7X11-inch baking pan coated with cooking spray.
Bake for 15-20 minutes or until stuffing is lightly browned.
Yield: 18 servings.

4.3. Deviled Eggs With Bacon Sriracha Avocado Filling

Ingredients:
12 eggs, hard boiled, peeled, halved lengthwise
6 slices low-sodium bacon, cooked crispy, drained, crumbled
1 Avocado, seeded, peeled
¼ cup Sriracha
½ cup whole egg mayonnaise
1 teaspoon Turmeric powder
2 limes juiced
Salt as you may desire
1 teaspoon sweet Hungarian Paprika

Directions:
Arrange halved eggs, yolk up, in a deviled eggs serving platter.
Remove the yolks to a food processor.
Add avocado, sriracha, mayonnaise, Turmeric, and lime juice to the food processor.
Pulse the processor to make a smooth yolk mixture paste.
Add salt as you may desire.
Pack blended yolk mixture into a pastry gun fitted with a fluted tip.
Fill each egg half with the mixture.
Swirl the tip as you squeeze to make a decorative filling.
Garnish with bacon crumbles.
Sprinkle paprika over all.
Makes 24 deviled eggs

4.4. Uncommonly Delightful Provençal Deviled Eggs

Ingredients:
1 tablespoon chopped sun-dried tomatoes, packed without oil
¼ cup boiling water
12 hard-boiled large eggs, shelled
⅓ cup Best Foods™ mayonnaise
1 tablespoon chopped pitted kalamata olives
2 teaspoons chopped fresh parsley
2 teaspoons chopped Mediterranean capers
½ teaspoon dried herbes de Provence
½ teaspoon Dijon mustard
¼ teaspoon finely ground Himalayan Pink salt
¼ teaspoon freshly ground white pepper
Chopped fresh parsley (optional)
Sweet Hungarian paprika

Directions:
Combine boiling water and tomatoes in a bowl.
Cover and let stand 30 minutes or until tender. Drain and set aside.
Cut eggs in half lengthwise and remove yolks to a medium mixing bowl.
Add tomatoes, mayonnaise, and next 7 ingredients (mayonnaise through pepper).
Using a fork, mash the ingredients to form a smooth paste.
Fill a pastry gun with the egg mixture and fill each egg half.
Dust with paprika and additional chopped parsley, if desired.
Makes 24 deviled eggs

4.5. Green Olives And Artichoke Hearts Tapenade

Ingredients:
10 large pitted green olives
3 tablespoons capers, drained
1 – 14 oz. can artichoke hearts, drained
1 tablespoon chopped fresh parsley
1 tablespoon fresh lemon juice
1 teaspoon Dijon mustard
½ teaspoon freshly ground black pepper
2 garlic cloves, minced
1 cup extra light olive oil
24 French baguette slices

Directions:
Add the olives, capers and artichoke hearts to a food processor. Pulse until chopped very fine.
Add the rest of the ingredients and pulse until finely chopped.
While pulsing, slowly drizzle in sufficient olive oil to make a thick Artichoke paste.
Spread paste on baguette slices and arrange on a serving platter.
Makes 24 appetizers.

4.6. Spanakopita Bites

Ingredients:
½ cup extra light olive oil
2 large onions, chopped
2 –10 oz. packages frozen chopped spinach - thawed, drained and squeezed dry
2 tablespoons chopped fresh dill
2 tablespoons all-purpose flour
2 – 4 oz. packages feta cheese, crumbled
4 large eggs, lightly whipped
Finely divided sea salt and freshly ground white pepper as you may desire
1½ packages phyllo dough
¾ lb. butter, melted

Directions:
Preheat oven to 350°F.
Heat oil to shimmering in a large saucepan over medium heat.
Stir-cook onions until translucent.
Mix in spinach, dill and flour.
Cook approximately 10 minutes, or until the moisture has evaporated somewhat.
Remove from heat and fold in cheese, eggs, and salt and pepper.
Place the stack of phyllo dough on a large work surface and cover with a moist piece of cheesecloth.
Separate one sheet of phyllo from the stack and evenly brush sheet with a light coating of butter.
Place another sheet of phyllo over the buttered sheet and press the two sheets together.
Cut the layered phyllo dough into long strips about 3 inches wide.
Repeat until all of the doubled phyllo sheets have been transformed into 3-inch wide strips.
Cover the pile of strips with a moist piece of cheesecloth.

Lay out one strip of phyllo at a time on the work surface with one of the narrow ends close to you. Place a heaping tablespoon of filling 1 inch from the end closest to you.

Fold the bottom right corner over the filling to the left edge to form a triangle.

Fold the triangle up, bringing the point at the bottom left up to rest along the left edge.

Turn the lower left corner over to touch the right edge.

Continue turning the triangle over in this manner until you reach the end of the phyllo.

Repeat with the remaining filling and phyllo dough.

Place filled phyllo dough triangles on a large baking sheet and brush with the remaining butter.

Bake in the preheated oven until the phyllo is golden brown, 45 minutes to 1 hour.

4.7. Titaina

Ingredients:
2 tablespoons pine nuts
1 tablespoon Avocado oil
½ red bell pepper, cored, seeded, diced
½ green bell pepper, cored, seeded, diced
½ small sweet Spanish onion, diced
4 garlic cloves, pressed
1 – 14.5 oz. can peeled and diced tomatoes, drained
1 – 5 oz. can Solid Pack Albacore Tuna, drained
½ teaspoon white cane sugar
¼ teaspoon ground Saigon cinnamon
1 pinch ground nutmeg
Finely divided sea salt and freshly ground white pepper as you may desire
Ritz® Crackers, for serving

Directions:
Stir-cook the pine nuts in a dry skillet over medium heat for about 5 minutes, or until fragrant.
Remove from heat and pour toasted nuts into a serving bowl and set aside to cool.
Heat oil to shimmering in a large, deep-sided skillet over medium heat.
Add the red and green bell peppers, and onion.
Stir-cook until peppers are soft and onion is translucent.
Add the garlic and stir-cook 30 seconds.
Stir in the tomatoes, and stir-cook for 15 minutes.
Break up the tuna and fold in the remaining ingredients (except crackers).
Simmer for about 15 more minutes.
Stir in the reserved toasted nuts.
Spread mixture on Ritz® crackers, arrange crackers on a serving tray, and serve.

4.8. Tortilla Espanola

Ingredients:
3 tablespoons extra light olive oil, divided
2 large Yukon potatoes, thinly sliced
Himalayan Pink Salt and freshly ground white pepper as you may desire
¼ teaspoon smoked paprika
1 sweet Spanish onion, thinly sliced
6 large eggs, beaten
1 bunch chives, chopped
Toothpicks

Directions:
Preheat oven to 350°F.
In an ovenproof skillet over medium heat, bring 1 tablespoon of oil to shimmering.
Carefully place the potatoes into the hot oil.
Season with salt and pepper, and sprinkle with smoked paprika.
Pan-fry the potatoes, stirring and tossing occasionally, until they are just beginning to brown.
Stir in the onion, and stir-cook until the potatoes are slightly browned and onion is translucent.
Remove the potato-onion mixture to a 3 qt. mixing bowl.
Remove the skillet from the heat, and wipe clean with paper towels.
Add beaten eggs, 1 teaspoon of oil, and chives to the potato-onion mixture.
Blend all together.
Bring 1 tablespoon of oil to shimmering in the skillet over medium heat.
Gently spoon the egg-potato mixture into the hot skillet.
Reduce heat to medium-low, and use a wide spatula to release the omelet from the skillet.
Slide the skillet into the preheated oven.

Bake until the omelet is puffed and the top is golden brown, about 5 minutes.

A toothpick inserted into the center of the omelet should come out clean.

Cut the omelet into bite-sized pieces, pierce each piece with a toothpick and serve hot.

4.9. Spanish Pan-Fried Shrimp With Garlic

Ingredients:
¼ cup extra light olive oil
10 garlic cloves, pressed
½ teaspoon crushed red pepper flakes
1 pound (20/36) uncooked headless, tail-off shrimp, peeled and deveined
Lawry's® garlic salt as you may desire
2 tablespoons chopped fresh parsley as you may desire
toothpicks

Directions:
Heat olive oil in a 12-inch, non-reactive skillet over medium heat.
Add shrimp and stir-cook until opaque in color, about 3 minutes.
Add garlic and red pepper flakes, dust with garlic salt, and stir-cook for 2 more minutes.
Sprinkle with fresh parsley, impale each shrimp on a toothpick, and serve immediately.

5. Main Course Recipes

5.1. Standing Beef Rib Roast And Gravy

Ingredients:
7 lb. standing beef rib roast, rinsed, patted dry
⅛ teaspoon finely ground Himalayan salt
¼ teaspoon freshly ground black pepper
⅓ cup red wine (not cooking wine)
2 cups Swanson® Unsalted Beef Flavored Stock
¼ cup Wondra® flour

Directions:
Preheat the oven to 325°F.
Season the beef with the salt and black pepper.
Place the beef into a roasting pan, rib-side down.
Roast, uncovered, for 2 hours 20 minutes for medium-rare or until desired doneness.
Remove the beef to a cutting board and let stand for 20 minutes.
Spoon off any fat from the pan drippings.
Stir the wine into the pan and heat over medium-high heat to a boil.
Using a wooden spoon, stir to scrape up any browned bits from the bottom of the pan.
Reduce the heat to medium and cook for 5 minutes.
Pour the wine mixture through a fine mesh sieve into a 2-quart saucepan.
Whisk to dissolve the flour in the stock placed in a medium bowl.
Gradually whisk the stock mixture into the saucepan.
Cook and stir over medium heat until the mixture boils and thickens.
Season with additional salt and black pepper, as you may desire.
Serve the beef gravy with the beef.
Serves 8

5.2. Italian Style Chicken With Peas And Bacon

Ingredients:
8 skinless, boneless chicken thighs
⅓ cup lemon juice.
6 pieces smoked bacon, chopped
2 garlic cloves, thinly sliced
1 bunch spring onions, roughly chopped (see Note)
¾ cup low-sodium chicken stock
1 cup frozen peas
1 Green Giant® Fresh Little Gem Lettuce, roughly shredded
2 tablespoons shredded mozzarella cheese

Directions:
Wash chicken and rub with lemon juice.
Submerge chicken in cool water for 15 minutes. Rinse and pat dry.
In a large, non-reactive, deep-sided frying pan, fry the bacon over medium heat.
Remove the cooked bacon and retain the bacon renderings.
Add the chicken and brown on all sides.
Add the garlic and spring onions.
Stir-cook for about 30 seconds, just until the spring onion stalks are bright green.
Pour in the chicken stock and return the bacon to the pan.
Simmer, covered, for 20 minutes.
Chicken is cooked through when chicken easily releases from the bone.
Increase heat under the pan and add the peas and lettuce.
Cook, covered, until the peas are tender and the lettuce has just wilted.
Stir in the mozzarella just before serving.
Serves 6

Note: "Spring Onions" are sprouted garlic. These can be found typically in farmer's markets, but only in the Spring (hence the name). To replace the spring onions, use 2 green onion stalks and 1 garlic clove for each spring onion called for in the recipe. This recipe calls for a "bunch", which is usually consists of 6-8 spring onions.

5.3. Portuguese Christmas Leg Of Lamb

Ingredients:
1 – 2 lb. half leg of bone-in lamb, washed in salted water, rinsed, dried, trimmed
6 garlic cloves, minced
½ teaspoon garlic powder
3 tablespoons butter
1 teaspoon freshly ground white pepper
Portuguese Mateus wine

Directions:
Preheat oven to 400°F.
In a suitable mixing bowl, blend the garlics, butter and pepper to form a paste.
Spread the paste evenly over the leg of lamb.
Place lamb in a roasting pan and place it in the preheated oven.
Roast until an instant reading thermometer inserted in the meat away from the bone reports 150°F.
Baste with wine and the cooking juices.
Remove to a serving platter, cover, and let rest 10 minutes before slicing.

5.4. Pork Roast And Gravy

Ingredients:
2 tablespoons water
4 cloves garlic, minced
½ teaspoon ginger powder
½ teaspoon thyme
½ teaspoon coarsely ground black pepper
¾ teaspoon crushed Rosemary
2 tablespoons Avocado Oil
4 lb. pork loin roast, trimmed, rinsed, patted dry, tied with Butcher's twine
4 Fuji Apples, peeled, cored, and sliced
2 large yellow onions, thinly sliced
2 cups low-sodium chicken broth
½ cup orange juice
4 tablespoons Arrowroot powder dissolved in 1 tablespoon water

Directions:
Preheat the oven to 425°F.
In a medium mixing bowl, combine the first 6 ingredients (water through rosemary) and set aside.
Brush the roast with oil.
Rub spice mixture all over the roast.
Place the apples and onions in a 2 qt. mixing bowl. Add oil and toss to coat.
Place the apples and onions in the roasting pan.
Put the roast on top and place in oven, uncovered.
Bake for 10 minutes, then reduce heat to 350°F and continue to bake 1 ½ to 2 hours.
Once the internal temperature of the roast reaches 155°F, remove roast from oven.
Place on a serving platter and cover with tin foil and let rest for 5 minutes.

Using a blender or food processor, puree the apples and onions.
Pour the broth and orange juice into the heated roasting pan.
Use a wooden spatula to scrape up all the tasty brown bits.
Strain liquid into a 2 qt. saucepan.
Add the pureed apples and onions and heat to a rapid simmer.
Gradually whisk in some of the dissolved Arrowroot.
Stir and add more Arrowroot until the gravy achieves the desired thickness.
Remove the gravy from the heat and place in a gravy boat.
Remove the twine from the roast and slice into ½-inch slices.
Fan out the meat slices on a serving platter and serve with a side of gravy.
Serves 4

5.5. Greek Christmas Pork Roast

Ingredients:
2 lbs. pork shoulder, trimmed, butterflied, pounded to ½-inch thick.
Salt and freshly ground black pepper as you may desire
8 garlic cloves, minced
1 teaspoon garlic power
12 oz. Naxos graviera cheese, diced (substitute: Gruyere cheese, diced)
½ cup pistachios, coarsely chopped
Grated zest and juice of 1 lemon
½ cup extra light olive oil
2 cups dry white wine (drinking wine, not "cooking wine")
2 cups low sodium chicken broth
½ cup lightly toasted pine nuts, coarsely chopped
½ cup walnuts, coarsely chopped

Directions:
Preheat the oven to 400°F.
Wash and pat the meat dry with paper towels.
Place butterflied pork shoulder on a large cutting board.
Dust the meat with salt and pepper as you may desire.
Evenly spread with garlics, cheese, pistachios, pepper and lemon zest.
Tightly roll up and tie with Butcher's twine.
Rub the outside with more salt and freshly ground black pepper as you may desire.
In a 5 qt. Dutch oven bring the oil to shimmering over medium-high heat.
Sear the pork on all sides.
Add the wine and 1 cup of broth, cover, and transfer pot to the oven.

Using a remote reading instant thermometer, roast the shoulder until the thermometer reports an internal temperature of 160 °F.

Add more broth to keep the roast moist.

Remove from oven and drizzle with lemon juice. Return roast to oven.

When the thermometer reports an internal temperature of 170 °F, sprinkle with the chopped pine nuts and walnuts.

Remove all to a serving platter, cover, and let rest 15 minutes before slicing into rounds.

Using a wire bail, remove the nuts to a side dish and serve along with the sliced meat.

5.6. Spice Rubbed Pork Loin Roast

Ingredients:
1 tablespoon ground cumin (optional)
1 tablespoon golden brown sugar
2 teaspoons dark chili powder
1 teaspoon fennel seeds
2 teaspoons ground coriander
1 teaspoon ground cinnamon
1 teaspoon crushed red pepper flakes
1 teaspoon freshly ground black pepper
2 lbs. boneless pork loin roast, rinsed, patted dry
2 tablespoons Avocado Oil

Directions:
In a sealable shaker jar combine all the spices. Shake well to mix.
Use 2 tablespoons of this seasonings blend for this recipe.
Store remaining seasonings blend in the freezer for up to 6 months.
Preheat oven to 325°F.
Trim fat from pork roast.
Coat pork roast with Avocado Oil.
Rub 2 tablespoons seasonings blend over all surfaces of the pork roast.
Place roast on a rack in a shallow pan.
Roast until an instant reading thermometer registers 155°F.
Remove roast from oven.
Cover meat with foil and let rest 25 minutes.
Serves 8

5.7. How To Make The Most Delicious Turkey Ever

This is a traditional way to cook an unstuffed turkey.

A refrigerated fresh turkey must be brought to room temperature before cooking. Place the bird, sealed in its plastic wrap, in a pan until you are ready to cook. Unseal the bird, wash, rinse, pat dry with paper towels, and proceed to cook it.

Defrost a frozen turkey in the refrigerator for several days. Allow approximately 5 hours of defrosting for every pound. A 15 pound turkey, for example, will take 3 days in the refrigerator to defrost.

Remove the giblets and neck. remove any remaining pin feather stubs in the turkey skin. Liberally coat the inside of the cavity with lemon juice. Rub a small handful of salt all over the inside of the turkey. Rinse well. Pat the turkey dry with paper towels. Rub melted butter all over the outside of the turkey.

Place the unstuffed turkey **BREAST DOWN** on a V-shaped cooking rack placed inside a matching roasting pan. Cooking the turkey "breast down" means the skin over the breast will not burn and the juices from the cooking turkey will collect in both the cavity and the breast while cooking. The result is a bird that has the most succulent turkey breast imaginable.

Put the turkey in a preheated 400°F oven. Cook the bird at least 12 minutes for every pound. For a 15 lb. turkey, that's 3 hours. Cook the bird at 400°F for 1 hour. Reduce the heat to 350°F for the next 2 hours.

To brown the breast, during the last 20 minutes of cooking, remove the bird from its rack, and place the turkey, breast side up, back in the pan, and back in the oven. Cover the legs with foil to prevent burning.

Using a remote reading instant thermometer inserted deep into the thickest part of the turkey breast or thigh, cook until the thigh reports 175°F. The breast meat should be 160°F to 165°F.

Remove the turkey to a cutting board and tent with foil. Let the turkey rest for 25-40 minutes before carving.

5.8. Apple-Shallot Roasted Turkey

Ingredients:
1 – 10 to 12-pound turkey
2 tablespoons Extra Light Olive oil
2 tablespoons chopped fresh parsley, plus 3 sprigs
1 tablespoon chopped fresh sage, plus 3 sprigs
1 tablespoon chopped fresh thyme, plus 3 sprigs
1 teaspoon kosher salt
1 teaspoon freshly ground pepper
1½ pounds shallots, peeled and halved lengthwise, divided
1 tart green apple, quartered
3 cups water, plus more as needed

Directions:
Preheat oven to 475°F.
Place the turkey, breast-side up, in a rack in a large, foil-lined roasting pan.
Pat the turkey completely dry with paper towels.
Whisk together the oil, chopped parsley, sage, and thyme, salt and pepper in a small bowl.
Rub the herb mixture all over the turkey.
With fingers, loosen skin starting from the edges of the turkey's cavity.
With fingers, work the herb mixture under the skin and onto the breast meat.
Place herb sprigs, 6 shallot halves and apple slices inside the turkey's cavity.
Tuck the wing tips under the turkey.
Tie the legs together with Butcher's Twine.
Add 3 cups water to the pan.
Roast the turkey until the skin is golden brown.
Remove the turkey from the oven.
Cover just the breast with a double layer of foil, cutting as necessary to fit.

Scatter the remaining shallots in the pan around the turkey.
Reduce oven temperature to 350°F.
Continue roasting until a thermometer placed close to the thigh joint registers 165°F.
If the pan dries out, tilt the turkey and let roasting juices run out into the pan.
Add 1 cup water to the pan.
Transfer the turkey to a serving platter and tent with foil.
Let the turkey rest for 30 minutes.
Remove the string and carve.

5.9. Asian Spiced Christmas Turkey

Ingredients:
1 – 12-14 pound turkey, thawed and brined
2 cups mayonnaise
⅓ cup Sriracha chile sauce
2 tablespoons ground ginger
2 tablespoons garlic powder
Salt and freshly ground black pepper as you may desire
1 bunch Thai basil, rinsed
3-4 stalks lemongrass, washed
1 bunch scallions, washed
2-inch length of fresh ginger, peeled, Julienned
Single Foil Sheet
String Lift
PAM® Cooking spray

Directions:
Preheat the oven to 450°F.
Place a String Lift in the center of the Single Foil Sheet. Lightly PAM® the center of the Sheet.
Dry the turkey thoroughly with paper towels and center the bird on the String Lift.
Stuff the main and neck cavities with basil, lemongrass, scallions and ginger slices.
Fold the neck flap under the turkey.
Mix the mayonnaise, sriracha, ginger powder and garlic powder in a bowl.
Liberally coat the entire bird.
Dust with salt and pepper as you may desire.
Seal the turkey in the Single Foil Sheet.
Place foil-wrapped turkey in a roasting pan and put into oven.
Roast for approximately 10 minutes per pound (14 lb. bird will roast for 140 minutes)

Turkey is done when an instant reading thermometer inserted into the breast reads 160°F.

Open wrap during the last 20 minutes to allow the skin to brown.

Allow the turkey to rest, still wrapped, at least 30 minutes before slicing.

Use the String Lift to move the turkey to a suitable cutting surface.

5.10. Fried Turkey Breast And Gravy

Ingredients:
3 lbs. boneless turkey breast
¼ cup Avocado Oil

Brining Solution:
4 cups water
2 tablespoons salt
2 tablespoons golden brown sugar
¼ cup dry sherry wine
¼ teaspoon celery seed
¼ teaspoon black pepper ground
½ teaspoon garlic powder
½ teaspoon dried sage
½ teaspoon dried thyme
½ teaspoon dried rosemary

Gravy:
32 oz turkey broth (may substitute chicken broth)
2 carrots roughly chopped
3 stalks celery roughly chopped
1 large yellow onion roughly chopped
1 tablespoon garlic minced
1 teaspoon garlic powder
¼ teaspoon whole black peppercorns
1 bay leaf
1 sprig fresh rosemary
5 sprigs fresh thyme
5 fresh sage leaves, chopped
2 tablespoon sherry wine
3 tablespoon butter
3 tablespoon flour
½ teaspoon salt as you may desire

Directions:

Mix all ingredients for brining solution in a 1gallon zipper locked plastic bag.
Submerge turkey in the brining solution
Refrigerate brining turkey overnight.
Remove turkey from bring solution, rinse, and thoroughly dry turkey breast with paper towels.
Discard brining solution.
Preheat oven to 350°F.
Pour Avocado oil in a 6 qt Dutch oven and add breast.
Place Dutch oven, covered, in the oven.
Cook until the breast's internal temperature has reached 165°F.
Remove and allow to rest 20 minutes before slicing

Gravy:
Add first 12 ingredients (broth through butter) to a suitable stock pot.
Bring to a boil.
Reduce heat to simmer.
Cover and cook 1 hour or until vegetables are soft.
Discard solids and reserve liquid.
Add butter to a clean pot and melt over medium heat.
Blend in flour to make a light tan roux.
Add reserved liquid and salt.
Bring to a boil.
Simmer for 10 minutes to thicken and then serve.

5.11. Garlic And Herb Roasted Turkey

Ingredients:
9 lb. fresh turkey, giblets removed, washed and dried
PAM® Cooking spray

Dry Brine:
2 kosher salt
1 tablespoon sugar

Garlic and Herb Butter:
4 oz. (1 stick) unsalted butter, softened to room temperature
4 cloves garlic, minced
2 tablespoons minced parsley
2 tablespoons minced thyme
Kosher salt and pepper as you may desire

Stuffing:
4 sprigs thyme
2 cloves garlic, smashed
1 apple, cored and quartered
1 cup dry white wine
1 cup turkey or chicken stock

Directions:
Dry Brine:
Combine salt and sugar and rub all over the turkey.
Place the turkey in a suitable plastic sealable bag and refrigerate overnight.

Garlic and Herb Butter:
In a suitable mixing bowl, combine all the ingredients.

Turkey:
Remove the brined turkey from the refrigerator. Rinse and pat dry with paper towels.
Let the bird come to room temperature.
Preheat the oven to 450°F.

Place a Single Foil Sheet on the working surface.
Center the String Lift and PAM® the area where the bird will be placed.
Center the turkey on the String Lift.
Spread the herb butter all over chicken.
With your hands, work the butter under the skin and inside the cavity.
Stuff the cavity with the herbs, apple and garlic.
Fold up the Single Foil Sheet to make a boat around the turkey.
Pour the wine into the cavity.
Seal the bird in the Single Foil Sheet.
Place in oven and roast for 12 minutes per pound, or until a thermometer reads 165°F.
Remove the turkey from the oven and let it rest for 30 minutes to 1 hour.

5.12. Garlic Herb Bacon Wrapped Turkey Breast

Ingredients:
3 tablespoons sweet balsamic vinegar (at least 9 gms. sugar per serving)
2 tablespoons extra light olive oil
6 sprigs fresh rosemary (divided)
6 sprigs fresh thyme (divided)
2 tablespoons Montreal® steak seasoning
6 cloves garlic, crushed
½ teaspoon garlic powder
3-4 lb. boneless turkey breast
10 slices low-sodium bacon

Directions:
Preheat the oven to 400°F.
Chop 4 rosemary sprigs and 4 thyme sprigs, discarding any woody stems.
In a medium bowl combine balsamic vinegar and oil.
Add chopped herbs, steak seasoning, and garlics. Mix thoroughly.
Liberally coat the turkey breast on all sides with the herb spice mixture.
Arrange the two remaining sprigs of rosemary and thyme on top of the turkey breast.
Plait the bacon slices over the top of the turkey breast.
Fold bacon ends under breast.
Line a roasting pan with aluminum foil.
Place a wire rack in the pan.
Place the bacon-wrapped turkey on top of the wire rack.
Brush any extra herb spice on top of the bacon.
Place in the oven and bake until the turkey breast reaches 165°F.
Remove breast from oven, tent with foil, and let rest 30 minutes.
Remove and discard the two sprigs before carving.

5.13. Grilled Tuscan Style Turkey

Ingredients:
12-14 lb. fresh or thawed turkey
6 tablespoons unsalted butter, melted, divided
4 tablespoons chopped fresh parsley
1 tablespoon chopped fresh thyme
2 tablespoons chopped fresh rosemary
2 tablespoons lemon zest
1 tablespoon extra light olive oil

Directions:
Spatchcock the turkey by cutting out the backbone and breaking the breastbone.
Loosen the skin over the breast.
With your hands, work a tablespoon or two of butter in between the skin and breast meat.
In a medium mixing bowl, combine the herbs, lemon zest, and oil.
Rub the turkey all over with the herb mixture.
Let the coated bird rest, covered, for 1 hour at room temperature.
Preheat the grill to 425°F. Set the grill for indirect cooking.
Place the turkey on the indirect cooking grill section.
Close the cover and grill the turkey until the breast reaches 150°F and the thighs reach 165°F.
Baste the turkey with the rest of the melted butter.
Remove turkey from the grill to a suitable cutting board and tent with foil.
Let the turkey rest for 15-20 minutes before carving.

5.14. Indian-Spiced Turkey Breast

Ingredients:
2 – 1-lb. boneless, skinless turkey breasts
1 cup plain yogurt (or plain kefir)
1-inch length fresh turmeric, grated (or 2 teaspoons dried Turmeric powder)
1-inch fresh ginger, peeled, grated
1 tablespoon garam masala spice blend
2 tablespoons salt, divided
1 teaspoon black pepper
handful of fresh cilantro, chopped
juice of 2 limes, divided
1 tablespoon Avocado oil

Directions:
Wash the breasts with water.
Rub a mixture of 1 tablespoon salt and juice of 1 lime over breast surfaces.
Submerge breasts in cool water for 15 minutes.
Rinse under clear water. Pat dry.
Place the turkey breasts in a 9X13-inch glass baking dish.
Whisk together the yogurt and all remaining ingredients, except oil, to make a marinade.
Coat each breast on all sides with the marinade.
Cover the turkey with plastic wrap.
Let marinate fin the refrigerator or at least 4 hours, preferably overnight.
Remove the breasts from refrigerator and bring to room temperature.
Preheat oven to 400°F.
Heat the oil to shimmering in a 6 qt Dutch oven over high heat.
Remove the turkey breasts from the marinade.
Brown the turkey breasts on each side in the Dutch oven.
Arrange the browned breasts in the Dutch oven.
Place the Dutch oven, uncovered, in the oven.

Bake until the thickest part of the beasts reaches 165°F.
Remove breasts to a cutting board.
Tent with foil, and let the breasts rest 10 minutes before slicing and serving.

5.15. Lemon Rosemary Brined Turkey

Ingredients:
1–10-15 lb. turkey

Making The Brine:
8 quarts water
1 cup sugar
1 cup kosher salt
2 lemons, sliced
4 bay leaves
6 sprigs fresh rosemary

Roasting The Turkey:
4 cloves garlic, minced
½ teaspoon garlic powder
1 tablespoon sweet Hungarian paprika
½ teaspoon freshy ground white pepper
¼ cup ghee

Directions:
Place a large plastic bag in a large container,
Add the water, sugar and salt and stir until the sugar and salt are completely dissolved.
Add the lemon slices, bay leaves, rosemary and turkey.
Close the bag and squeeze out enough air so the turkey is completely covered with brine.
Place the bucket in the refrigerator.
Let the turkey soak in the brine for at least 18 hours and up to 36.
Preheat the oven to 450°F.
Remove the turkey from the brine, draining the cavities, and reserving the lemon slices and herbs.
Place a Single Foil Sheet on the working surface.
Center the String Lift and Pam the area where the bird will be placed.
Center the turkey on the String Lift.

In a small bowl, stir together the garlics, paprika, pepper and ghee until combined.

With your hands, rub this mixture all over the turkey, inside and out.

Stuff the lemon slices and rosemary sprigs inside the cavity.

Tie the turkey's legs together with Butcher's twine.

Roast the turkey at 10 minutes per pound (14 lbs. = 2 hrs 20 minutes).

The turkey is done when a thermometer placed in the thickest part of the thigh reads 180° F.

Let the turkey rest for 25 minutes before carving it.

5.16. Mother Mitchell's Turkey And Dressing

Ingredients:
10 lb. –14 lb. fresh (or completely thawed) turkey
1 lb. low-sodium bacon, cooked crispy, well-drained, chopped. reserve renderings.
2 medium-sized onions, chopped/diced
1–12 oz box Mrs. Cubbison's original dressing mix®
1– 7 oz can jumbo black olives, drained, chopped
1– 14 oz. can sweet corn, drained
1 cup hearts of celery, chopped
1 – 14 oz. can low sodium turkey broth
4 eggs, hard boiled, shelled and chopped
3 raw eggs to hold mixture together
¼ lb. salted creamery butter, melted,
Salt
Turkey String Lift

Directions:
Sauté onions in bacon renderings.
Drain onions and let cool.
In large pot, mix all ingredients except turkey, broth, butter, and salt.
Fold in just enough turkey broth to make stuffing stick together when made into a ball.
Rub salt all over bird and into all cavities.
Rinse bird with fresh cool water and pat dry with paper towels.
Stuff turkey with dressing.
Place Turkey String Lift along centerline of single sheet of tinfoil and place bird in center of string.
Rub butter over skin on outside.

ROASTING PROCEDURE:
Seal stuffed bird in **a single sheet of tinfoil** .
Roast stuffed bird in preheated 450°F oven for 2½ hours (instant thermometer should read 155°F or higher).

Open foil and let bird brown, another 25 minutes.
Remove bird from oven, reseal foil, and let rest 45 minutes before carving.
Bird's temperature will rise another 5-10 degrees as it rests.
165°F is the optimum temperature; bird could be overcooked at higher temperatures.

5.17. Turkey And Yam Shepherd's Pie

Ingredients:
4 tablespoons butter, divided
2 ½ pounds orange yams, washed and dried
1 large Vidalia onion, peeled, diced
2 large carrots, peeled and diced
2 stalks celery, chopped
2 tablespoons finely chopped fresh thyme
2 teaspoons finely chopped fresh rosemary
2 pounds ground turkey
¼ cup tomato paste
½ cup golden brown sugar
2 tablespoons all-purpose flour
2 tablespoons Worcestershire sauce
2 cups low-sodium chicken broth
4 oz. cream cheese
1 large egg, scrambled
Freshly ground white pepper
10 ounces fresh or frozen peas

Directions:
Preheat the oven to 400°F.
Place the washed yams on an ungreased cookie sheet.
Place the cookie sheet in the preheated oven.
Cook the yams until the skin is wrinkled and a fork comes out clean.
Reduce the oven temperature to 375°F.
Cool the yams and peel and discard skins.
Place the peeled yams in a large bowl.
In the bowl with the yams, add the sugar, cream cheese, egg, and 2 tablespoons butter.
Add salt and pepper as you may desire.
Using an immersion blender, thoroughly blend all ingredients.
Heat a 4 qt Dutch Oven over medium-high heat.

Melt 2 tablespoons butter in Dutch Oven.
Add the ground turkey.
Stir-fry the mixture until the turkey is no longer pink.
Use a wooden spatula to break up clumps.
Add the onions and sauté until translucent.
Add the carrots, celery, thyme and rosemary and toss to blend.
Stir-cook 2 minutes until fragrant.
Blend in the tomato paste, flour and Worcestershire sauce.
Whisk until well-mixed then add the chicken broth.
Bring to a boil, then reduce heat and simmer on medium heat.
Stir-cook until a thick sauce forms, then add the peas.
Pour the turkey mixture and sauce into a lightly greased 2 quart baking dish.
Spread the yam mixture over the top. Mound as desired.
Bake until lightly browned, about 35 minutes.
Serves 6

6. Side Dishes And Condiments

6.1. Broiled Asparagus With Lemon-Shallot

Ingredients:
1 lb. thin asparagus spears, trimmed
4 teaspoons Avocado oil, divided
Salt and freshly ground black pepper as you may desire
½ small shallot, minced
2 teaspoons fresh lemon juice
1 teaspoon grated lemon zest
1 tablespoon minced fresh tarragon
¼ teaspoon Dijon mustard
1 tablespoon water

Directions:
Preheat broiler.
Place oven rack in top position, about 4 inches from heating element.
Arrange the asparagus in a single layer on a foil-lined cookie sheet.
Drizzle with 2 teaspoons oil
Season with salt and pepper as you may desire.
Roll spears to coat with oil blend.
Broil, about 8–10 minutes, until asparagus spears are tender and lightly crisped.
Using a fork or tongs, roll spears over after 4 minutes.
Transfer to serving platter.
In a small bowl, whisk together the rest of the ingredients and the rest of the oil.
Drizzle over cooked asparagus.
Season with salt and pepper as you may desire.
Serve hot.
Serves 4

6.2. Roasted Asparagus With Caper Dressing

Ingredients:
1 bunch asparagus, trimmed
2½ teaspoons extra-virgin olive oil, divided
⅛ teaspoon salt
¼ teaspoon freshly ground pepper, divided
2 small shallots, peeled
2 tablespoons flat-leaf parsley leaves
1½ tablespoons Mediterranean capers, rinsed
1 tablespoon white-wine vinegar

Directions:
Preheat oven to 450°F.
Arrange asparagus in a single layer in a rimmed, foil-lined baking pan.
Drizzle the asparagus with 1½ teaspoons oil, salt
Dust with ⅛ teaspoon pepper, toss to coat, and arrange evenly.
Roast until the asparagus begins to lightly crisp.
Using the back of a wooden spoon, roll the asparagus over after about 4 minutes.
Transfer roasted asparagus to a rimmed serving platter.
Combine shallots, parsley, capers, vinegar, oil, and pepper in a food processor.
Pulse to coarsely chop and mix all together. Pour over the asparagus.
Serve warm.

6.3. Broccoli Bake

Ingredients:
1 lb. sweet ground sausage
2 cups fresh broccoli florets
8 oz. Ricottacheese
1 cup shredded cheddar cheese
1 – 4 oz. can chopped mushrooms
2 large eggs
1 teaspoon low sodium baking powder
2 packages Pillsbury® crescent rolls
1 tablespoon butter, melted, divided

Directions:
Preheat oven to 350°F.
In a non-reactive frying pan, Stir-cook the sausage unit no longer pink.
Use a wooden spatula to break up clumps. Drain as desired.
Microwave the broccoli in a microwaveable bowl with a bit of water. Drain.
In a 3 qt. mixing bowl, combine sausage, broccoli, and the rest of the ingredients.
On an unfloured work surface, roll out the crescent rolls.
Mound a tablespoon or two of the sausage mixture in the center of one of the crescent rolls.
Leave about a half inch border around the edges.
With your finger, wet the border.
Cover with the other sheet of crescent roll.
Pinch the two sheets together to form a pocket around the sausage mixture.
Place on an ungreased cookie sheet.
Brush with a thin layer of the butter.
Place sausage roll in the oven and cook until golden brown.
Brush on another layer of butter while hot.
Serves 4

6.4. Broccoli And Beef Short Ribs

Ingredients:
2 lbs. beef short ribs
1 large onion, sliced
2 cups water
2 medium sized tomatoes, quartered
1 medium head broccoli, washed, loosely chopped.
2 pack sinigang mix
3 miniature hot banana peppers

Directions(Instant Pot®):
Wash the meat to remove excess fat and any bone chips.
Place meat in the Instant Pot®.
Add water, chopped onions, tomatoes, sinigang mix packet, fresh peppers.
Close and lock the lid. Set the vent to "Sealing."
Select "Pressure Cook," High pressure, 45 minutes.
When the display shows "L010," perform the QR method to release any residual pressure and steam.
Wait until the pressure indicator pin drops down.
Carefully open and remove the lid.
Add another packet of sinigang mix.
Add broccoli and close and seal lid, setting the vent to "Sealing"
Select "Pressure Cook", High pressure, 0 minutes, "Warm" off.
When the display shows "Off," perform the QR method to release pressure and steam.
Wait until the pressure indicator pin drops down.
Carefully open and remove the lid.
Serve.

Tip: Use pork or chicken instead of beef. Combine pork, beef, chicken as a pleasant variation.

6.5. Chinese Style Broccoli

Ingredients:
½ tablespoon plus ½ teaspoon canola oil
3 cups fresh broccoli florets
1 tablespoon low-sodium soy sauce
1 garlic clove, minced
1 teaspoon fresh lemon juice

Directions:
Heat oil in a well-seasoned wok over medium-high heat.
Add broccoli and stir-fry about 3 minutes.
Add the rest of the ingredients.
Stir-fry until broccoli is crisp-tender, about 4 minutes.
Serve hot.
Serves 2

6.6. Roman Style Broccoli

Ingredients:
1 head broccoli, cut into florets, stems peeled and sliced
1 teaspoon plus 1 tablespoon extra light olive oil
2 tablespoons whole-wheat Panko-style breadcrumbs, original flavor
5 garlic cloves, thinly sliced
⅓ cup sweet white dinner wine(not "cooking" wine - too salty)
⅛ teaspoon crushed red pepper flakes
Coarsely ground Sea salt
Zest of ½ lemon

Directions:
Steam the broccoli in a large pot of salted boiling water until just bright green, about 3 minutes. Cool under cold running water and pat dry with paper towels.
In a non-reactive saucepan, heat 1 teaspoon oil over medium-high heat.
Fold in the Panko breadcrumbs and stir until they are lightly toasted, 2 to 3 minutes.
Remove to a serving bowl and set aside.
Heat the remaining 1 tablespoon oil in a large skillet over medium-high heat.
Add the garlic slices and stir-fry 30 seconds
Stir in the wine, pepper flakes and reserved broccoli.
Sprinkle with salt and stir-fry until the wine has evaporated, about 5 minutes.
Arrange broccoli mixture in a serving bowl and sprinkle with the toasted Panko and lemon zest.

6.7. Balsamic-Braised Bacon Brussels Sprouts

Ingredients:
5 Brussels Sprouts, halved
2 strips center cut bacon, cooked, drained, and crumbled. Reserve renderings.
4 tablespoons Sweet Balsamic Vinegar (at least 9 gms. sugar per serving), divided
Extra Light Olive oil, divided
Finely ground Himalayan Salt and freshly ground pepper as you may desire
1 egg, fried sunny side up

Directions:
Preheat oven to 400°F.
Place halved Brussels sprouts in an 8X8-inch glass baking dish.
Drizzle oil and 2 tablespoons balsamic vinegar to coat.
Toss with bacon crumbles.
Dust with some salt and pepper as you may desire.
Toss to coat.
Bake in oven for about 20 minutes.
Drizzle remaining oil and vinegar and toss to coat.
Stir in 1 teaspoon bacon renderings.
Bake an additional 10 minutes.
Top with fried egg and serve warm.

6.8. Bang Bang Brussels Sprouts

Ingredients:
3 tablespoons extra-light olive oil
2 tablespoons sweet Filipino chili sauce
1 tablespoon Sambal Oelek
Juice of 1 lime
4 cloves garlic, minced
½ teaspoon garlic powder
2 lb. Brussels sprouts, trimmed and halved (quartered if large)
Kosher salt and freshly ground white pepper as you may desire

Directions:
Preheat oven to 425°F.
In a 3 qt. mixing bowl, whisk together oil, chili sauce, Sambal Oelek, lime juice, and garlics.
Add Brussels sprouts and toss to coat.
Spread coated Brussels sprouts in a single layer on a foil-lined rimmed baking pan.
Pour any remaining sauce over the sprouts and dust with salt and pepper as you may desire.
Roast until Brussels sprouts are slightly charred and tender, 30 to 35 minutes.

6.9. Roasted Brussels Sprouts With Garlic Aioli

Ingredients:
For Brussels Sprouts:
1 lb. Brussels Sprouts, trimmed
2 tablespoons extra light olive oil
½ teaspoon finely ground Himalayan salt
½ teaspoon freshly ground black pepper
1 sprig fresh rosemary
1 large shallot, minced

For Garlic Aioli:
2 garlic cloves, crushed, minced
1 large egg
1 tablespoon freshly squeezed lemon juice
½ teaspoon finely ground Himalayan salt
¼ teaspoon freshly ground white pepper
1 teaspoon Hungarian Sweet ("edes") Paprika
½ cup extra light olive oil
1 tablespoon snipped chives

Directions:
Roasted Brussels Sprouts:
Preheat oven to 400°F.
Trim the Brussels Sprouts, removing any yellow or damaged outer leaves.
Slice Brussels Sprouts in half lengthwise.
In a 2 qt. mixing bowl, combine the oil, shallot, rosemary, salt and pepper.
Add Brussels Sprouts and toss to coat.
Arrange the Brussels Sprouts in a single layer on a foil-lined, rimmed baking pan.
Roast until Sprouts' outsides are crisped and the insides are still tender.
As they crisp, turn Sprouts over.

Sprinkle with more salt as you may desire, and remove to a serving bowl.

Garlic Aioli Dipping Sauce:

Add the Aioli ingredients (except oil and chives) to a blender.

While blending at low speed, drizzle in the oil to form a pale yellow sauce.

Transfer sauce to a small dipping bowl.

Garnish with chives and serve alongside the Brussels Sprouts.

6.10. Brussels Sprouts And Toasted Pecans

Ingredients:
Sauce:
3 tablespoons Cream Sherry Vinegar
2 tablespoons water
1 tablespoon Dijon Mustard
¼ cup minced shallots
¼ teaspoon freshly ground black pepper
¼ cup Extra Virgin Olive Oil

Vegetables:
1 lb. fresh Brussels Sprouts, trimmed and halved lengthwise
½ cup Pecan halves, split lengthwise

Directions:
Preheat oven to 400°F.
In a food processor, blend together vinegar, water, mustard, shallots, and black pepper.
With processor on low, drizzle in oil in a slow, gentle stream.
Arrange Sprouts and pecans in an oven-proof casserole dish.
Pour sauce over Sprouts and pecans.
Toss to coat.
Cook, covered, for 25 minutes or until Sprouts are beginning to caramelize.
With a wooden spoon, lightly toss to coat Sprouts with the heated sauce and pecans.
Serve immediately.
Serves 4

6.11. Easy Brown Sugar Glazed Carrots

Ingredients:
16 oz. baby carrots, washed, drained
2 tablespoons butter
⅓ cup golden brown sugar, packed
1 cup water
Finely ground Himalayan salt and freshly ground black pepper as you may desire

Directions:
In a medium saucepan, combine the carrots, butter, brown sugar, and water.
Bring to a boil over high heat.
Stir to dissolve sugar and to combine all the ingredients.
Reduce heat to a gentle rolling boil.
Cook until carrots are soft and glazed, and liquid has evaporated.
Removed glazed carrots to a serving bowl.
Dust with salt and pepper as you may desire.
Serves 4

6.12. Simple Glazed Carrots

Ingredients:
4 medium carrots
2 tablespoons butter
2 tablespoons golden brown sugar
fresh mint leaves or thyme, optional

Directions:
Wash, and peel carrots.
Slice carrots on the bias into elliptical coins.
Cook carrots in boiling salted water until tender. Drain.
Add sliced carrots to a non-reactive saucepan.
Stir in butter and sugar.
Stir-cook over medium-high heat until carrots are slightly browned and glazed.
Blend in a teaspoon of chopped fresh mint leaves or thyme, as desired.
Remove to a serving bowl.
Serves 4

6.13. Gingered Carrots

Ingredients:
1lb. carrots, peeled, sliced into 4-inch lengths and Julienned
3 tablespoons unsalted butter
2 tablespoons dark brown sugar
2 teaspoons powdered ginger
Salt and freshly ground white pepper as you may desire

Directions:
Place carrots in a saucepan and cover with water.
Bring to a boil and cook until tender.
Drain well. Clean out he saucepan.
Return carrots to the saucepan.
Add the rest of the ingredients and bring to a boil.
Cook until most of the liquid has evaporated and carrots are glazed.
Serve immediately, spooning the sauce over the carrots while serving.
Serves 4

6.14. Garlicky Mashed Cauliflower

Ingredients:
1 large head of elephant garlic
1 teaspoon extra light olive oil
1 head cauliflower (separated into florets, woody stems discarded)
2 teaspoons fresh thyme (chopped)
½ teaspoon kosher salt as you may desire
¼ teaspoon freshly ground white pepper as you may desire

Directions:
Preheat oven to 410°F.
Peel away and discard the dried outer layers of garlic skin, leaving bulb intact.
Slice enough skin off the top of the bulb to expose the tops of the individual cloves.
Place the trimmed garlic bulb upright in a ramekin.
Brush the exposed cloves with oil, making sure the entire top is thinly coated.
Cover with foil and bake for 35 minutes. The garlic cloves should feel soft and squishy.
Remove ramekin from oven and let cool until comfortable to handle.
Squeeze the roasted garlic out of the cloves into a 2 qt. mixing bowl.
In a microwave steamer, place sufficient water and the cauliflower florets.
Steam the florets until they are fork-tender. Drain and discard liquids.
Transfer the florets to the mixing bowl with the garlic. Add the thyme and oil.
With an immersion blender, mash all together to a smooth consistency.
Add more oil until the mixture reaches your desired consistency.

Remove to a serving bowl.
Season with salt and pepper as you may desire.
Serves 4.

6.15. Sweetest Corn On The Cob

Ingredients:
¼ cup white sugar
1 tablespoon lemon juice
6 ears corn on the cob, stripped husks retained and silk discarded

Directions:
Cover the inside bottom of a large pot with washed corn husks.
Fill about ¾ full of water and bring to a boil.
Stir in sugar and lemon juice, dissolving the sugar.
Gently arrange ears of corn into the pot on the husks.
Cover the pot and remove from heat.
Let the corn steep in the hot water for 15 minutes.
Remove corn from water, shaking off the excess, and arrange on a serving platter.

6.16. Cranberry Conserve

Ingredients:
1 lb. fresh cranberries, washed
1 cup water
¾ cups cane sugar
1 whole Navel orange, peeled, chopped
1 Fuji apple, cored, peeled, diced
1 Bartlett pear, cored, peeled, diced
1 cup golden raisins
1 tablespoon fresh lemon juice
¾ cup coarsely chopped pecans

Directions:
In a medium heavy saucepan combine cranberries and water.
Stir-cook until cranberries burst, about 10 minutes.
Fold in all other ingredients, except pecans.
Stir-cook until mixture thickens, about 25 minutes.
Gently blend in pecans. Remove to a serving bowl.
Using a wooden spoon, stir all together.
Allow mixture to cool.
Serves 6

6.17. Classic Green Bean Casserole

Ingredients:
2-10 ¾ oz. cans condensed Cream of Mushroom Soup
1 cup whole milk
2 teaspoons low sodium soy sauce
¼ teaspoon freshly ground white pepper
4 packages [9 oz. each] frozen green beans, thawed, thoroughly dried on paper towels
2⅔ cups French's® French Fried Onions, divided

Directions:
Preheat oven to 350°F.
In 3 qt. casserole, combine soup, milk, soy sauce and pepper. Mix well.
Stir in beans and 1⅓ cup French's® Fried Onions.
Bake, uncovered, in oven for 25 minutes.
Stir contents to blend ingredients.
Sprinkle with remaining French's® Fried Onions.
Bake 5 more minutes or until onions are golden.
Serves 12

6.18. Savory Green Beans With Caramelized Onions

Ingredients:
2 tablespoons lard
1 large sweet Vidalia or Mayan onion, thinly sliced
¼ cup golden brown sugar
3 tablespoons butter
4 cloves garlic, minced
½ teaspoon garlic powder
1 lb. green beans, trimmed, rinsed, blanched, thoroughly dried on paper towels
½ cup low-sodium chicken broth
Kosher salt as you may prefer
1 teaspoon freshly ground black pepper
1 cup shredded white mild Cheddar

Directions:
Heat lard to shimmering in a sauce pot over medium-high heat.
In a 2 qt. mixing bowl, toss onions with sugar to coat.
Add coated onions to pot and stir-fry until caramelized.
Remove caramelized onions to a serving bowl and set aside.
In a 12-inch, deep sided, covered skillet over medium-high heat, melt butter.
Stir in the two garlics and stir-cook 30 seconds.
Fold in green beans, chicken broth and ½ of the caramelized onions.
Season with salt and pepper as you may desire.
Stir all together, cover, and cook until beans are crisp-tender, 10 minutes.
Uncover and sprinkle cheese over all.
Cover while cheese melts. Uncover and mix the melted cheese into the beans.
Top with the remaining caramelized onions.
Serve immediately.

6.19. Green Beans With Pine Nuts And Mozzarella

Ingredients:
2 tablespoons pine nuts
8 ounces green beans, trimmed
8 ounces yellow wax beans, trimmed
1 tablespoon extra-virgin olive oil
¼ teaspoon finely ground sea salt
⅛ teaspoon freshly ground black pepper
4 oz. block of fresh part-skim mozzarella cheese
¼ cup basil leaves, sliced

Directions:
Heat the oven to 300°F.
Spread pine nuts on a baking sheet and toast until fragrant and lightly golden, 5 to 7 minutes.
Set aside.
Steam the beans in a saucepan using a steamer insert.
Rinse beans in a colander under cold running water until cool to the touch.
Drain beans and pat very dry with paper towels.
Transfer beans to a medium mixing bowl.
Toss with oil, salt, and pepper.
Thinly slice cheese into 8 slices.
On each of 4 salad plates, place a cheese slice.
Arrange a layer of green beans, followed by a layer of yellow beans.
Top with another slice of cheese.
Add another layer of beans.
Sprinkle each salad mound with basil and pine nuts and serve.
Serves 4

6.20. Italian-Style Green Beans

Ingredients:
2 tablespoons Avocado oil, divided
8 oz. pork loin, cut into bite-sized pieces
2 Roma tomatoes, cored, seeded, diced
4 cloves garlic, crushed, minced
1 lb. fresh Chinese long green beans, cut into 2-inch lengths
1 – 4 oz. can pitted small black olives, drained
½ small yellow onion, thinly sliced, quartered
1 tablespoon dry Italian Seasoning
¼ teaspoon crushed red pepper flakes
Salt and freshly ground black pepper as you may desire

Directions:
In a non-reactive pot, heat oil to shimmering then add pork.
Stir-cook until pork is no longer pink and cooked through.
Add onions and stir-cook until onion is translucent.
Fold in tomatoes and garlic and stir-cook for 30 seconds.
Blend in the rest of ingredients.
Toss to mix, then cover and simmer 20 minutes or until beans are cooked as you may desire.

6.21. Easy Hot Potatoes

Ingredients:
6 large Yukon potatoes, peeled, diced
1 can cream of mushroom soup
Velveeta hot pepper cheese, cubed
Garnishes:
Sliced Jalapeno peppers, sliced black olives, thinly sliced green onions

Directions:
Preheat oven to 350ºF.
In a 3 qt. casserole dish, mix all ingredients.
Bake, uncovered, for 30 minutes.
Using a wooden spatula, blend the casserole's contents.
Return to oven and bake an additional 30 minutes.
Use a fork to pierce potatoes and check for tenderness.
Bake an additional 30 minutes or until potatoes test fork tender.
Top with garnishes as you may desire.
Serve.
Serves 4.

6.22. Mustard Mashed Potatoes

Ingredients:
6 -8 Yukon gold potatoes, skin on, scrubbed
4 garlic cloves, crushed, minced
1 sprig fresh thyme
Water as necessary
1 pint whole milk
1 pint heavy whipping cream
4 oz. butter, melted
salt and freshly ground white pepper as you may desire
2 tablespoons coarse grain mustard

Directions:
Add potatoes garlic, and thyme to a large, non-reactive soup pot.
Pour in enough water to just cover.
Bring to a boil and cook until potatoes are fork-tender.
Drain potatoes and garlic in a colander and transfer to a 3 qt. mixing bowl.
Using an immersion blender, mash potatoes and garlic.
Drizzle in the milk and cream until the potatoes reach the desired consistency.
Add butter and salt and pepper as you may desire.
Fold in mustard.
Serves 6

6.23. Savory Mashed Potatoes

Ingredients:
1 large head of garlic
Extra light olive oil
1 teaspoon garlic powder
3 lb. Yukon potatoes, peeled, and cut into 1-inch cubes
1 cup whole milk
¼ cup butter, melted
Salt as you may desire
½ teaspoon freshly ground white pepper

Directions:
Preheat oven to 410°F.
Peel away and discard the dried outer layers of garlic skin, leaving bulb intact.
Remove between ¼ and ½ -inch off the top of the bulb, exposing the tops of the individual cloves.
Place the trimmed garlic bulb upright in a ramekin.
Brush the exposed cloves with oil, making sure the entire top is thinly coated.
Dust the exposed cloves with garlic powder
Cover with foil and bake for 35 minutes. The garlic cloves should feel soft and squishy.
Remove from oven and let cool.
When cool enough to be handled, squeeze the garlic into a 3 qt. mixing bowl.
Add the milk, butter, salt, and pepper. Set aside.
Bring a large pot of water to a rolling boil.
Add potatoes and boil until fork-tender.
Using a wire bail, drain potatoes and add them to the mixing bowl. Discard cooking water.
With an immersion blender, mash the potatoes together with the roasted garlic.

Add more melted butter until they reach your desired consistency.
Add salt and pepper as you may desire.
Remove to a serving bowl.

6.24. Baked Yam Casserole

Ingredients:
3 lb. large orange yams, unpeeled
1 cup brown sugar
Butter, melted
1 package baby marshmallows
1 jar Maraschino cherries, drained, stems removed

Directions:
Preheat the oven to 350°F.
Bake the yams until fork tender.
Remove yams, slice open, and scrape flesh into a 3 qt. serving bowl.
Fold in brown sugar and enough butter to make a smooth mixture.
Dot top with marshmallow and cherries.
Return to oven and heat through. Marshmallows will melt slightly and brown.

Hint: Don't heat in casserole in the microwave: the marshmallows will expand to a runny mess!

7. Special Desserts

7.1. Apple Frangipane Tart

Ingredients:
1 – 9-inch pie crust
4 ounces almond paste
¼ cups sugar
¼ cups all-purpose flour
3 tablespoons butter (brought to room temperature)
2 large eggs
½ teaspoons almond extract
¼ cups unsweetened applesauce
5 apples (such as Granny Smith, Honey Crisp, or Golden Delicious, or a combination of them)
Juice of ½ of a large lemon
3 tablespoons butter, divided
2 tablespoons sugar, divided
¼ cups sliced almonds

Directions:
Preheat oven to 375°F.
Fit the pie dough into a non-stick springform baking pan.
Press the dough into the bottom and sides and trim any excess. Set aside.
In a food processor, combine the almond paste and sugar.
Pulse until thoroughly blended.
Add the flour and butter and pulse to form a thick paste.
Add the eggs, almond extract and applesauce and pulse until smooth.
Spread filling across the pie crust and chill for up to 30 minutes.
On a cutting board, core, peel and slice all of the apples into ½ - inch thick slices, lengthwise.

Remove the sliced apples to a 5 qt. mixing bowl and squeeze the lemon juice all.
Toss to coat.
In a 12-inch, deep-sided, non-reactive skillet melt 2 tablespoons butter.
Add the apples and 1 tablespoon sugar.
Sauté the apples until they just begin to soften and become pliable.
Remove from heat and let the apples cool for 10 minutes.
Melt the remaining tablespoon of butter in a small ramekin and set aside.
Arrange the cooled apples in concentric circles in the pie crust.
Start at the rim of the pie crust and work toward the center.
Use thinner slices of apple to curl into tighter rosettes as you approach the center.
Lightly brush the apples with the melted butter.
Sprinkle with the remaining sugar and scatter the sliced almonds over all.
Place filled pan on a rimmed, non-stick baking pan and place in the oven.
Bake until apples and crust are browned.
Remove from oven and place on a wire cooling rack.
When cooled to room temperature, remove pan to a serving platter and remove the outer rim.
Optional: slide the tart off the pan's bottom onto the serving platter.
Serve at room temperature.

7.2. Nectarine Almond Frangipane Tart

Ingredients:
Pastry Dough:
1 cup all-purpose flour
3 tablespoons sugar
½ teaspoon salt
¾ stick cold unsalted butter, cut into ½-inch pieces
½ teaspoon finely grated fresh lemon zest
2 large egg yolks
½ teaspoon Madagascar vanilla
1½ teaspoons water

Frangipane Filling:
7 to 8 oz almond paste (not marzipan or almond filling)
½ stick unsalted butter, softened
3 tablespoons sugar
⅛ teaspoon almond extract
2 large eggs
3 tablespoons all-purpose flour
½ teaspoon salt
1 ¼ lb. firm-ripe nectarines, washed, dried, pitted, sliced into ¼-inch thick slices, lengthwise

Glaze:
⅓ cup peach preserves
2 tablespoons water
1 tablespoon Disaronno® Amaretto (optional)

Directions:
Make Dough Shell:
Put oven rack in middle position and preheat to 375°F.
Pulse flour, sugar, and salt in a food processor to combine thoroughly.
Add butter and zest and pulse until slightly lumpy.
Add yolks, vanilla, and water and pulse just until a clumpy dough begins to form.

Turn dough out onto a floured work surface and knead for 40 strokes.

Divide the dough into 4 portions and form each portion into a ball.

Using a French roller, flatten each ball into a rectangle.

Put each dough rectangle in a springform tart pan.

Using well-floured fingers, pat out to make an even layer over bottom of the tart pan.

Stretch the dough so it extends about ¼ inch above rim. Chill 30 minutes.

Lightly prick tart shell all over with a fork, then add a pie weight chain to each shell.

Bake shell until golden around edge, about 15 minutes.

Return pans and carefully remove the pie chains.

Return pans to the oven and bake until shell is golden all over, about 15 minutes more.

Remove pans from oven and cool on a wire cooling rack.

Make Filling:

Using a food processor, pulse together almond paste, butter, sugar, and almond extract until creamy.

Add eggs, 1 at a time, and pulsing to incorporate.

Pulse in in flour and salt to make the frangipane filling.

Divide and spread frangipane filling evenly in the four tart shells.

Stand the nectarine slices, skin sides down, decoratively on the filling in each pan.

Be careful not to push the slices too far down into the filling.

Bake tarts until frangipane is puffed and golden and edges of nectarines are golden brown, about 1 ¼ hours.

Make Glaze:

In a medium saucepan over moderately-high heat add the preserves and water.

Using a wooden spatula, stir-cook until preserves are melted and solids are crushed and blended.

Remove from heat and force the mixture through a chinois, discarding any solids.

Stir in Amaretto (if using).

Finish Tart:

Brush top of hot tart generously with glaze and cool in pan on a wire rack for at least 15 minutes.

Remove tarts from the springform pans and let tart cool completely.

7.3. Orange Coconut Pecan Pie

Ingredients:
1 prepared pie crust
5 tablespoons unsalted butter
1¼ cups packed light brown sugar
¾ cups light corn syrup
2 teaspoons vanilla extract
1 Navel orange, zested
¼ teaspoons salt
3 large eggs
1 cup coconut shreds
2½ cups whole pecans

Directions:
Preheat oven to 350°F.
Place an oven rack to the center of the oven.
Place the pie crust on a lightly floured work surface.
Using a French rolling pin, roll the crust until it is 12-inches across.
Arrange the crust in a 9-inch pie pan, draping the excess over the edges.
Fold the excess crust over to form a rim.
Using the tines of a fork, form a decorative crimp along the rim.
Prick the bottom of the shell several times with the fork tines.
Cover with plastic wrap and refrigerate until the filling is ready.
In a medium saucepan over medium heat, stir-cook the butter and sugar together until blended.
Remove from heat and blend in the corn syrup, vanilla, orange zest and salt. Set aside.
In a 3 qt. mixing bowl, using an immersion blender, beat the eggs until frothy.
Add the sugar mixture and coconut and beat until smooth.
Fold in the pecans.
Place the pie pan on a foil-lined, rimmed baking pan.

Carefully fill the shell with the pecan mixture and level with a silicone spatula.
Bake for 25 minutes, then rotate the pan 180° to brown evenly.
Bake for another 25 - 35 minutes until filling is set.
If the rim starts to get too brown, cover the rim with a little aluminum foil.
Remove pie to a wire cooling rack and cool to room temperature.
Serve.

7.4. Roasted Pears With Dark Chocolate Hazelnut Sauce

Ingredients:
2 Bosc pears, halved, cored
3 tablespoons melted coconut oil, divided
½ cup chopped hazelnuts, divided
¾ cup unsweetened vanilla almond milk (or milk of choice)
2 tablespoons cacao powder (80% cacao or higher)
1 tablespoon maple syrup
¼ teaspoon finely ground Himalayan salt

Directions:
Preheat oven to 400º F.
Place pears cut side down in a baking dish.
Drizzle with 1 tablespoon coconut oil.
Bake until tender and golden brown, 35-45 minutes.
Add remaining coconut oil, ¼ cup hazelnuts and the remaining ingredients to a food processor.
Pulse until smooth, using a silicone spatula to scrape sides as needed. Set aside.
Arrange cooked pears, cut side up, in a serving dish.
Drizzle chocolate sauce over the pears.
Sprinkle with remaining hazelnuts before serving.
Serves 2

7.5. Pecan Pie Cobbler

Ingredients:
1 box Pillsbury® refrigerated pie crust, softened as directed on box
½ cup butter, melted
2½ teaspoons Madagascar vanilla
1 cup white cane sugar
2½ cups of Dark Karo Syrup
6 eggs, slightly beaten
2 cups coarsely chopped pecans or 2 cups pecan halves
Butter-flavor cooking spray
Non-dairy whipped topping (optional)

Directions:
Pre-heat oven to 350°F.
Coat the inside of a 13x9-inch clear glass baking dish with cooking spray
Remove 1 pie crust from pouch and unroll on unfloured work surface.
Using a French Rolling pin, roll into 13x9-inch rectangle.
Repair places that may have become torn.
Place the crust in the glass baking dish, spreading the edges to fit in the corners.
In large bowl, blend together the next 6 ingredients.
Pour half of filling into the crust-lined baking dish, leaving a ¼" clean strip all around the edge.
Remove second pie crust from pouch and unroll on unfloured work surface.
Using a French Rolling pin, roll into another 13x9-inch rectangle.
Place the second crust over the first, pinching the edges to seal.
Pour the rest of the filling over top of the crust.
Arrange on the central rack in the oven.
Cook 40-50 minutes until the filling is set.
Remove to a cooling rack.

When cool, score with a wetted sharp knife and serve.
Top each piece with a dollop of non-dairy whipped topping.

7.6. Strawberry Surprise Cake

Ingredients:
1 commercially prepared Angel food Cake
2 – 8 oz. containers fresh Strawberries (more if needed)
1 large container Cool Whip®
1 can strawberry frosting

Directions:
Place Angel food cake upside down on plate.
Slice off top approximately ½-inch below top.
Using fingers, tear out the insides of the cake in 1-inch pieces, leaving a ½-inch wall around the outside and bottom.
Fill in hole in bottom of cake with pieces of torn-out cake.
Clean strawberries and remove green leaves.
Select 10 large, well-formed strawberries and set aside.
Slice the remaining strawberries into thin wafers.
In a 4 qt. mixing bowl, place the torn-out pieces and the strawberries. Gently fold in the Cool Whip®. Fill the angel food cake cavity with the strawberry-cake-Cool Whip® mixture.
Put the cake top on, fill hole with mixture and cover all with frosting.
Halve the set-aside strawberries and arrange on the top as a crown.
Serves: 6-8

7.7 Very French Cherry Dessert

Ingredients:
¾ lb. graham crackers, finely crushed
1 cup melted butter
¼ cup white cane sugar
2 cups powdered sugar
8 oz. cream cheese
1 large tub Cool Whip™, more if desired
1 can cherry pie filling

Directions:
Preheat oven to 350°F.
In a 2 qt. mixing bowl, combine crushed graham crackers, butter, and cane sugar.
Evenly spread a 13x9-inch glass baking dish with cracker mixture and bake for 5 minutes.
Remove to a wire cooling rack to cool.
Whip together the powdered sugar and cream cheese.
Fold the Cool Whip™ into the cream cheese mixture.
Spread mixture evenly over cracker crumb base.
Top with cherry pie filling and use a silicone spatula to smooth evenly.
Refrigerate several hours or overnight.
Top with more Cool Whip™, as desired.

Bonus Recipe Section

To all of you who took the time to seek out this book, Many Thanks!

As promised, this special recipe section is a compendium of recipes culled from our previous books, and some recipes that have never been published, nor may ever be published again.

These special recipes are our very own signature meals that we personally prepare for only a few of our extraordinary friends. But as you have taken the item to seek out our "**Effortless Christmas Feast Planning!**," and knowing how busy you all are, we have decided to share these with you.

Most people are afraid to make a mistake, either in cooking or in life. To them, we say, "Try it! Make something that you've never tried before. Don't worry if it turns out not to your liking, or as if you thought it should. Go ahead! Try it again!!"

We never worry about throwing out something that has failed: we just go out, get more ingredients and try again. That's the only way you'll learn.

Some of these seemingly easy recipes here are the result of many hours of failed experiments. But the end results have been amazing! Look at what you're holding in your hands.

So, go ahead. Try your hand at it. After all Paris wasn't built in a fortnight!!

Enjoy them in good health!

Warmly,

Arroz Caldo

Ingredients:
2 lbs. chicken (thighs or drumsticks), remove bones, cut into bite-sized pieces
1 teaspoon. salt
1 tablespoon Avocado oil
3 cloves garlic, crushed
½ teaspoon garlic powder
thumb-sized fresh ginger, peeled and finely sliced
2 cups uncooked rice, washed and drained
7 cups water
3 tablespoons fish sauce
4 sliced green onions, for garnish
4 tablespoons fried garlic, for toppings
5 limes (or calamansi), cut into wedges
Low-sodium soy sauce

Directions:
Rub chicken pieces with salt, wash and drain.
Submerge chicken in cool water for 15 minutes. Drain and set aside.
Heat oil to shimmering in a non-reactive cooking pot over medium heat.
Add chicken and stir-cook until lightly browned. Remove from heat; set aside.
In the pot, add the uncooked rice and water; bring to a boil.
Reduce the heat to simmer and fold in the chicken, garlic and ginger.
Season with fish sauce.
Cover and simmer until rice is cooked to your liking.
If arroz caldo is too thick, add a little water.
Serve arroz caldo in individual serving bowls.
Squeeze some fresh lime (or calamansi) juice, as desired, over top.

Garnish with sliced green onions, fried garlic and lime wedges. Serve with a side of soy sauce and fish sauce.

Divine Chicken Divan

Ingredients:
1 lb. chicken breast
Juice of 1 lemon
1 tablespoon avocado oil
2 cups leek diced
½ teaspoon Himalayan salt or as you may desire
5 tablespoons flour
1 can low-sodium chicken broth
1 cup nonfat milk
½ teaspoon dried thyme
½ teaspoon freshly ground black pepper or as you may desire
2 – 12 oz. bags fresh broccoli florets
1 cup reduced fat Parmesan cheese, grated
¼ cup reduced fat mayonnaise
2 teaspoons Dijon mustard

Directions:
Preheat oven to 375°F.
Wash chicken with lemon juice, then submerge chicken in cool water for 20 minutes.
Place chicken in a 5qt. Dutch oven.
Add just enough water to cover chicken and bring to a boil.
Reduce heat to simmer and simmer until chicken is no longer pink.
Remove chicken to a cutting board and slice chicken into 1-inch chunks.
Discard any excess fat and small bones.
Discard water from Dutch oven and wipe dry with paper towels.
Heat Dutch oven until water drops sizzle. Add oil, leek, and salt and cook until soft.
Add flour, chicken broth, milk, thyme and pepper and bring to a boil.
Reduce heat and add broccoli and simmer 3 minutes.

Remove from heat and stir in one half of the Parmesan cheese, all the mayo and mustard.
In a 3 qt. Corningware® casserole, put in half of the broccoli mixture
Top with the cooked, cubed chicken, then top with last of the broccoli mixture.
Sprinkle the remaining Parmesan cheese on top.
Bake for 20 minutes.
Serves 6

Parisienne Chicken And Rice Bake

Ingredients:
1 tablespoon sweet Hungarian Paprika
⅛ teaspoon hot Hungarian Paprika
1 teaspoon freshly ground black pepper
1 –10 ¾ oz. can Cream of Mushroom Soup
4 oz jar sliced mushrooms with liquid
2 cups water
1 cup sour cream
½ cup sherry
1 cup uncooked Basmati long-grain rice
6 skinless, boneless chicken breasts, excess fat and small bones removed
Juice of 1 lemon

Directions:
Preheat oven to 375°F.
In a small bowl, blend the paprikas with the pepper.
In a 2 qt. shallow baking dish, blend the next 6 ingredients (soup through rice) with 1 teaspoon paprika mix.
Wash the chicken with the lemon juice. Submerge the chicken in cool water for 15 minutes.
Remove chicken and pat dry with paper towels
Arrange chicken on rice mixture.
Sprinkle chicken with the rest of the paprika mix.
Cover and bake for 90 minutes or until chicken is well done, rice is fully cooked, and liquid is absorbed.
Uncover the last 30 minutes to let the chicken brown.
Remove chicken and rice to separate serving bowls.
Fluff rice with fork.
Serve warm.
Serves:6

Garlic Seasoned Vegetables

Ingredients:
1¾ cups low-sodium chicken broth
2 cloves garlic, minced
¼ teaspoon garlic powder
4 cups fresh cut-up vegetables of your choice (broccoli, celery, peppers, carrots, etc.)

Directions:
Bring the broth, garlics and vegetables to a boil in a 3-quart saucepan over medium-high heat. Reduce the heat to simmer. Cover and simmer until the vegetables are tender-crisp.
Using a wire bail, remove the vegetables to a serving bowl.

Hungarian Goulash With Yellow Onions

Ingredients:
2 lb. beef, cut into ¾-inch cubes
2 large yellow onions, thinly chopped
1 tablespoon Avocado oil
1 tablespoon butter
3 cups low sodium beef bouillon
2 tablespoons Hungarian Sweet Paprika
½ teaspoon Hungarian Hot Paprika
6 cloves garlic, crushed, minced
Freshly ground black pepper as you may desire
Lawry's® Garlic Salt as you may desire

Directions:
Heat the oil to shimmering in a 5 qt. Dutch oven over medium-high heat.
Using a wooden spoon, sauté the beef in batches.
Remove browned beef to a serving bowl.
Add the butter and onions and stir-cook the onions until caramelized.
Remove from heat and stir in garlic and paprikas.
Stir-cook until the paprikas are fragrant.
Return Dutch oven to medium heat and add beef and beef broth.
Bring to a boil, then lower heat to simmer.
Cover and cook until meat is fork tender.
Adjust seasonings and serve
Serves 4

Pork Estofado

Ingredients:
1½ lb. pork tenderloin, cut into bite-sized pieces
½ cup low- sodium soy sauce
¼ cup Heinz® Apple Cider vinegar
3 cloves garlic, minced
2 tablespoons brown sugar
1 medium onion, sliced into rings
1 tablespoon crushed red peppers
Extra Light Olive Oil, for frying
½ cup low-sodium chicken broth
1– 8 oz. can Contadina® tomato sauce
½ cup whole black olives, pitted (optional)
2 pcs. cooked Chinese sausage, sliced on the bias
1–8 oz jar pimiento, cut into strips

Directions:
In a plastic zipper-closure freezer bag, combine pork and the next 6 ingredients(soy sauce through peppers).
Squeeze the air out, seal, and knead to mix the marinade and to coat the pork.
Refrigerate for an hour or overnight.
Heat oil in a non-reactive, deep walled skillet over medium heat.
Remove pork from marinade. Reserve marinade.
Stir-fry the pork until no longer pink. Remove meat to a serving bowl.
Retain ¼ cup oil and discard the rest.
Return meat, reserved marinade and broth to the pan.
If necessary, add a little more broth to just cover the meat.
Bring to a boil, then lower heat to simmer and simmer, covered, 20 minutes.
Uncover and fold in tomato sauce, olives, Chinese sausage and pimiento.
Cook, covered, until pork is tender.

Transfer all to serving dish.
Serve.

Roasted Shiitakes And Pacific Cod

Ingredients:
2 pounds shiitake mushrooms, stems removed, sliced
4 tablespoons extra light olive oil, divided
4 sprigs fresh rosemary
4 Pacific cod or halibut fillets (6 to 8 ounces each)
1 tablespoon fresh lemon juice
1 tablespoon Dijon mustard
Kosher salt and freshly ground white pepper as you may desire

Directions:
Preheat oven to 450°F.
In a medium mixing bowl, toss mushrooms with 2 tablespoons oil and rosemary.
Arrange coated mushrooms on a large rimmed, aluminum foil-lined baking pan.
Dust with salt and pepper as you may desire.
Tossing them occasionally, roast mushrooms until tender and browned.
Separate the mushrooms to the sides of the pan.
Place cod in center of pan and dust cod with salt and pepper as you may desire.
Turn cod over and dust the other side.
Roast the cod until opaque throughout.
Remove cod and mushrooms to a serving platter.
In a small mixing bowl, whisk together remaining oil, lemon juice, and mustard.
Dust with salt and pepper as you may desire.
Serve as a dipping sauce with the cod and mushrooms.
Serves 4

10. About the Authors

Part 2

Introduction

Welcome and thank you for downloading my ebook!

You will surely adore each recipe here from its first to last as they will for sure astonish you with new flavours and all have clickable links in the table of contents so it's easy to find them.

1. Beef Pot Roast With Turnip Greens

Ingredients
3.4 ounces all-purpose flour (about 3/4 cup)
1 (3-pound) boneless chuck roast, trimmed
1 teaspoon kosher salt
1/2 teaspoon freshly ground black pepper
1 tablespoon olive oil
1 pound fresh turnip greens, trimmed and coarsely chopped
3 cups (2-inch) diagonally cut parsnips (about 1 pound)
3 cups cubed peeled Yukon gold potatoes (about 1 pound)
2 cups cipollini onions, peeled and quartered
2 tablespoons tomato paste
1 cup dry red wine
1 (14-ounce) can fat-free, lower-sodium beef broth
1 tablespoon black peppercorns
4 thyme sprigs
3 garlic cloves, crushed
2 bay leaves
1 bunch fresh flat-leaf parsley
Thyme sprigs (optional)

Instructions

Place flour in a shallow dish. Sprinkle beef evenly with salt and pepper; dredge in flour. Heat a large skillet over medium-high heat. Add oil to pan; swirl to coat. Add beef; sauté 10 minutes, turning to brown on all sides.

Place turnip greens in a 6-quart electric slow cooker; top with parsnips, potatoes, and onions. Transfer beef to slow cooker. Add tomato paste to skillet; cook 30 seconds, stirring constantly. Stir in wine and broth; bring to a boil, scraping pan to loosen browned bits. Cook 1 minute, stirring constantly. Pour broth mixture into slow cooker.

Place peppercorns and next 4 ingredients (through parsley) on a double layer of cheesecloth. Gather edges of cheesecloth together; secure with twine. Add cheesecloth bundle to slow cooker. Cover and cook on LOW 8 hours or until beef and vegetables are tender. Discard cheesecloth bundle.

Remove roast from slow cooker; slice. Serve with vegetable mixture and cooking liquid. Garnish with thyme sprigs, if desired.

2. Cinnamon Roll Casserole

Ingredients
2 12 oz tubes of cinnamon rolls cut into quarters- divided
4 eggs
1/2 cup whipping cream
3 Tbsp maple syrup
2 tsp vanilla
1 tsp cinnamon
1/4 tsp nutmeg

Instructions
Spray your crock with cooking spray.
Place a layer of cinnamon roll pieces to cover the bottom of your slow cooker completely. (Reserve icing packets)
Beat eggs, cream, maple syrup, vanilla and spices until blended well.
Pour evenly over the rolls in the slow cooker.
Place remaining roll pieces on top and spoon one packet of icing evenly over rolls.
Cover and cook on low for 2½ to 3 hours or until sides are golden and rolls are set.
Drizzle remaining icing over top and serve warm.

3. Slow Cooker Glazed Ham

Ingredients
1 fully cooked ham (any size will work as long as you have a slow cooker large enough for it)
sauce
1 1/4 cups brown sugar
1/4 cup honey
1/4 cup spicy brown mustard
3/4 cup dr. pepper (half of a can)
1/4 cup maple syrup

Instructions
Score ham by using a sharp knife to cut lines into ham in a criss cross pattern. The lines only need to be about ⅛th of an inch deep. Fill slow cooker with about 1 inch of water. Place ham in slow cooker. Cover and cook on low for 4-6 hours.
An hour before serving, prepare the sauce. Whisk together all sauce ingredients in a medium sauce pan. Bring to a boil, then reduce to a simmer and cook for 10 minutes. Remove from heat and allow to thicken for 5-10 minutes.
Drain water and ham juices from slow cooker. Pour sauce over ham inside the slow cooker, being sure to cover the whole ham. Cover and cook another 30 minutes. Place ham on serving dish. Carve/slice the ham and spoon the remaining sauce from the slow cooker over the ham.
Serve warm. Enjoy!

4. Sweet And Spicy Cranberry Meatballs

Ingredients

Meatballs
2 pounds ground beef
22 saltine crackers, crushed
1/3 cup dry minced onion
2 eggs, beaten
1/2 cup milk
2 teaspoons ground ginger
1 teaspoon salt
1/4 teaspoon pepper
2 teaspoon garlic powder

Sweet and Spicy Cranberry Sauce
14 oz. can whole cranberry sauce
1/4 cup quality hoisin sauce like Kikkoman or Lee Kum Kee
1/4 cup ketchup
2 tablespoons red wine vinegar
2 tablespoons soy sauce
2 teaspoons-2 tablespoons Franks Buffalo Hot WINGS Sauce*
1 teaspoon garlic powder
1/2 teaspoon ground ginger
2 tablespoons brown sugar

Instructions

Preheat oven to 400F degrees. Place a baking rack on top of a baking sheet. Set aside. (If you don't have a baking rack, line baking sheet with parchment paper.)

In a large bowl, combine all of the meatball ingredients, mix until well combined. Roll meat mixture into desired meatball size**. Place meatballs onto prepared baking sheet and bake for 5 minutes, or until lightly browned.

Meanwhile, add all of the Sweet and Spicy Cranberry Sauce ingredients starting with just 2 teaspoons hot wings sauce to a bowl and mix to combine. You can add more hot sauce to taste at the end of cooking.

Line the bottom of your slow cooker with meatballs, then a layer of Sweet and Spicy Cranberry Sauce, then the remaining meatballs followed by the remaining. Sauce. Gently stir meatballs an hour after cooking.

Cover and cook on low heat for 2 hours. Taste and stir in additional hot wings sauce (I use a total of 2 tablespoons which is spicy) Keep warm until serving.

5. Slow-Cooker Falling-Off-The-Bone Short Ribs

Ingredients
5 pounds beef short ribs
Kosher salt and freshly ground black pepper
3 tablespoons dried thyme
2 tablespoons dried rosemary
1/4 cup ground porcini mushrooms/dried mushroom powder
1/4 cup all-purpose flour
Olive oil
3 celery stalks, chopped
2 large Spanish onions, chopped
3 medium carrots, peeled and chopped
1 medium fennel bulb, trimmed, cored, and chopped
6 garlic cloves, chopped
2 cups red wine, such as Cabernet Sauvignon
3 tablespoons tomato paste
3 cups chicken stock, homemade preferably
Bouquet garni of 1 bay leaf, 6 thyme sprigs, 6 parsley sprigs, and 1 small rosemary sprig, tied together with kitchen twine

Instructions
Place the short ribs in a large stockpot filled with water and bring to a boil. Boil the short ribs for 5 minutes. Drain and discard the water. (This helps remove the fat.)
Pat dry the ribs thoroughly with a paper towel. Season the ribs with salt and pepper.
Combine the dried thyme, dried rosemary, ground porcini mushrooms and flour in a bowl.
Place a large sauté pan over medium heat. Lightly coat the bottom of the pan with olive oil. Dredge the ribs in the porcini mixture. Brown the ribs in batches until the ribs are browned on all sides, about 15 minutes. Transfer the ribs to the insert of a 6 1/2-quart slow cooker.
Pour off most of the fat from the sauté pan. Brown the celery, onions, carrots, and fennel in batches, about 7 minutes per

batch. Season each batch with salt and pepper. Add the garlic to the last batch and cook for 3 minutes more, until the garlic is very fragrant and slightly softened. Do not overbrown the garlic.

Transfer the browned vegetables to the insert. Add the wine and the tomato paste to the sauté pan. Stir together with a wooden spoon or spatula to break up the tomato paste. Gently scrape the pan to gather up the browned bits.

Transfer the wine to the insert. Add the stock and bouquet garni. Cover and cook on Low for 10 hours.

Remove the short ribs from the insert and place them on a platter. Tent loosely with foil to keep them warm. Pour the braising liquid through a fine-mesh strainer into a saucepan. Discard the vegetables and bouquet garni. Skim the fat off the liquid. Reduce over high heat by one half, or until the liquid is thick and coats the back of a spoon, about 10 minutes. Pour the sauce over the ribs.

Serve with your choice of accompaniment like grits, rice, polenta or potatoes.

6. Slow-Cooker Triple Chocolate Brownies

Ingredients
2 1/2 cups packaged brownie mix
1/2 cup milk chocolate chips
1/2 cup packed brown sugar
1/2 cup very hot water
2 eggs, beaten
3 tablespoons butter, melted
1 package (2 3/4 ounces) instant chocolate pudding mix
2 tablespoons unsweetened cocoa powder
Whipped cream or ice cream (optional)

Instructions
Coat inside of slow cooker with nonstick cooking spray.
Combine brownie mix, chocolate chips, brown sugar, water, eggs, butter, pudding mix and cocoa in slow cooker; stir to blend. Cover; cook on high for 2 hours.
Turn off heat. Let stand 30 minutes. Top with whipped cream, if desired.

7. Christmas Slow Cooker Whole Chicken

Ingredients
1 Whole Roaster Chicken 4-5 pounds
2 Cups of Milk
2 Cups of Fresh Whole Cranberries
1.5 large Oranges
2 Whole Cinnamon Sticks
Salt and Pepper as desired

Instructions
Prepare whole chicken for cooking by removing neck and any organ packages that were included. Clean and pat dry with paper towel. Cut one half of a large orange into two quarters and stuff the chicken with it. Tie the wings back. Take your whole large orange and cut into slices.

Add milk and place chicken breast side down in the slow cooker. Sprinkle salt and pepper over the entire exposed chicken. Pour the cranberries over the top, allowing for some to rest on the chicken. Place some of the orange slices on top and place the extras surrounding the chicken.

Add cinnamon sticks over the top. Cook on low for 6 hours or until ready. Recommended to use a pop up thermometer to make sure the internal temperature is 165°F (per FoodSafety.org).

Once chicken is cooked, carefully move the chicken to an oven safe casserole dish. Carry the cranberries and oranges over with only little juice. Discard the cinnamon sticks. Broil the chicken for about 10 minutes or until the skin is a nice crispy brown. Let rest for about 10 minutes before serving. Enjoy!

8. Ham Steaks And Pineapple Rings

Ingredients
2.5 lbs ham, sliced into 1/2 inch slices (you can use more or less ham)
20 ounce can Pineapple Slices (juices reserved for sauce)
6 ounce can Maraschino Cherries, drained
3 tablespoons Brown Sugar, packed
1 tablespoon Mustard
1 tablespoon Apple Cider Vinegar

Instructions
Add ham slices, pineapple slices, and maraschino cherries to the slow cooker.
Put reserved pineapple juice, brown sugar, mustard, and apple cider vinegar in a medium sized bowl.
Whisk until smooth, and pour over ham, pineapple and cherries in the slow cooker.
Cover, and cook for 5 hours on LOW, with out opening the lid during cooking time.
Drizzle sauce over each serving. ENJOY!

9. Turkey Breast And Gravy

Ingredients
3-6 lb. Boneless Turkey Breast (I trimmed off the excess skin that was hanging over the sides of the turkey)
2 (1.25-oz.) pkgs. dry turkey gravy mix
1 (10.75-oz.) can cream of chicken soup
1 3/4 cups water
1/4 tsp. dried thyme
1/8 tsp. black pepper

Instructions
In a medium-sized bowl whisk together the gravy mix, can of soup, water, thyme and pepper until smooth. Pour this mixture into a 6-quart or larger slow cooker.
Add the turkey breast into the gravy mixture.
Cover and cook on LOW for 5-6 hours without opening the lid during the cooking time.
Remove the turkey on to a cutting board and slice.
Stir the gravy and serve!

10. Nutella French Toast Casserole With Caramelized Bananas

Ingredients
1 loaf challah bread (about 1 pound), cut into cubes
6 large eggs
2 cups vanilla almond milk (or normal milk)
1 teaspoon ground cinnamon
1 tablespoon vanilla extract
2 heaping tablespoons Nutella, plus more for topping
Pinch salt
1 tablespoon unsalted butter
4 bananas, sliced
1 tablespoon brown sugar

Instructions
Cube your bread and place it in the slow cooker.
Add the eggs, milk, cinnamon, vanilla extract, Nutella, and salt to a bowl and whisk to combine.
Pour over the challah bread in the slow cooker.
Mix so that all of the bread is saturated with the mixture.
Cover and cook on HIGH for 2 hours. (NOTE: depending on the size and heat of your slow cooker, this time may have to be adjusted. Check every hour hour, mixing for even cooking)
When there are about 15 minutes left on the slow cooker, slice your bananas and add to a bowl.
Add the brown sugar and mix to combine.
Add the butter to a saute pan over medium high heat. Add the banana slices to the pan (you may have to work in batches) and cook for about 2 minutes on each side or until the bananas have browned slightly.
Scoop out the French Toast mixture and top with a scoop of the bananas. Add a dollop of Nutella if desired.

11. Slow-Cooker Turtle Monkey Bread

Ingredients
2/3 cup packed brown sugar
1/2 cup butter
1/4 cup granulated sugar
1 can (16.3 oz) Pillsbury™ Grands!™ Homestyle refrigerated buttermilk biscuits
3/4 cup pecan halves
2 tablespoons whipping cream
1/3 cup milk chocolate chips

Instructions
Spray 4 1/2- to 5-quart slow cooker with cooking spray. In 2-cup microwavable measuring cup, mix brown sugar and butter; microwave uncovered on High 1 to 2 minutes, stirring every 30 seconds, until mixture is boiling and smooth.

In large resealable food-storage plastic bag, place granulated sugar. Separate dough into 8 biscuits; cut each into fourths. Add a few of the biscuit pieces at a time to bag; shake to coat.

Sprinkle 1/4 cup of the pecans in slow cooker; top with half of the biscuit mixture. Pour one-third of the butter mixture over biscuits in cooker. Repeat with 1/4 cup pecans and remaining biscuit mixture. Pour remaining butter mixture over biscuits, and sprinkle with remaining 1/4 cup pecans.

Cover; cook on High heat setting 1 1/2 to 2 hours or until knife inserted in center comes out clean and biscuits are no longer doughy in center. Tops of biscuits will be moist and may appear unbaked. Turn off cooker.

Carefully remove cover so condensation does not drip onto bread. Cover opening with paper towels; return cover to cooker. Let stand 10 minutes. Run a knife around edge of cooker; turn bread upside down onto heatproof serving plate.

In 1-quart saucepan, heat cream over medium heat just to boiling. Remove from heat. Stir in chocolate chips until melted and smooth. Drizzle over monkey bread. Serve warm.

12. Slow Cooker Christmas Cocoa

Ingredients
1 1/2 cups heavy whipping cream
(1) 14-ounce can sweetened condensed milk
6 cups milk
2 teaspoons vanilla
2 cups of chocolate chips
1 teaspoon pure mint extract

Instructions
Gently stir the ingredients together and cook on low for 1.5 to 2 hours.
Using a soup ladle, pour the hot cocoa into holiday mugs and top with generous amounts of ingredients such as whipped cream, marshmallows, and crushed peppermint patties.
Include candy canes instead of spoons for stirring

13. French Toast Casserole

Ingredients
1 loaf of sliced bread
6 eggs
2 cups milk
1/2 tsp cinnamon

Topping
1/4 cup butter, softened
1/2 cup packed brown sugar
1 tsp cinnamon
1/2 cup chopped pecans
dash of nutmeg

Instructions

Whisk eggs, milk, and cinnamon together then pour over diced bread in a large bowl. Let this soak overnight in the fridge or for at least 4 hours.

When ready to bake, grease the slow cooker and pour in the bread mix. Mix together the butter, brown sugar, cinnamon, pecans and nutmeg then crumble and cover the top of the mix. Cover and cook for 4 hours on low.

Let rest for 15-20 minutes then chow down!

14. Slow Cooker Christmas Pudding

Ingredients
300g dried fruit of your choice (include some citrus peel if liked)
80ml Tia Maria
75g soft butter
75g soft dark brown sugar
50g plain flour
1/2 tsp cinnamon
1/4 tsp cloves
1/2 tsp baking powder
60g breadcrumbs
1 large egg plus 1 large egg yolk
1 small-medium Bramley apple, coarsely grated
1 tbsp honey, golden syrup or treacle as preferred

Instructions

If you have time, soak the dried fruits of your choice in the Tia Maria. A week is great but you can speed up the process by heating the fruits and booze in a bowl covered with cling in the microwave for 15-30 seconds. Allow to cool back to room temp before using and they will have plumped and absorbed the liqueur.

Butter a 1.5 pint pudding basin. Plastic or ceramic are perfectly fine.

Beat the butter and sugar then beat in the eggs and honey or syrup. Sift over the flour, spices and baking powder then stir in the bread crumbs. Mix in your dried fruits, the grated apple and any residual alcohol. Scrape the lot into the pudding basin and cover with a piece of buttered grease proof paper and square of foil you have folded an inch wide pleat into. (Making sure the paper is next to the pudding batter.)

Tie the foil in place under the rim of your basin with string crimping any residual foil and paper around this to prevent leakage of water into the pudding.

Place the pudding in your slow cooker and pour in boiling water from the kettle upto 1-2 inches from the rim of the pudding basin. Put the lid on and cook on low for 8 hours.

When cooked remove from the slow cooker and cool to room temperature. Replace the grease proof, foil and string then store somewhere cool and dark until Christmas Day. Reheat in the slow cooker in the same manner as which you cooked it, this time 3-4 hours steaming will suffice but more is unlikely to cause a problem should you need or want to delay serving dessert for a longer period of time.

15. Slow Cooker Candy Cane White Hot Chocolate

Ingredients
1/2 gallon whole milk (8 cups)
2 (4-oz.) pkgs Ghiridelli white chocolate baking bars, broken up into small pieces
1/2 cup crushed candy canes or starlight candies
1/2 tsp. vanilla
whipped cream for serving (I use Reddi-Whip)
more crushed candy canes for garnish

Instructions
Add the milk, broken up white chocolate, crushed candy canes, and vanilla to a 5-quart or larger slow cooker.
Cover, and cook on HIGH for 1.5 hours (stirring every 15 minutes).
Serve topped with whipped cream and topped with crushed candy canes for garnish.

Raspberry Almonds Squares

- Prep Time -10 mins
- Cook Time-40 mins
- Ready In-50 mins

Ingredients

- 1 tbsp ground flax seeds
- 3 tbsp very warm water
- 2½ cups almonds
- ⅓ cup maple syrup
- ⅓ cup coconut oil, melted or very soft
- 1 tsp pure vanilla extract
- ¼ tsp salt
- 1 cup raspberry jam of your choice (see notes above)
- ½ cup sliced almonds

Directions

1. Preheat oven to 350F. Line an 8x8 baking dish (or anything of a similar size) with some parchment paper.
2. Make a flax egg by mixing the ground flax in warm water in a small cup. Stir and set aside to gel for a few minutes.
3. Process almonds in a food processor until ground just slightly coarser than almond flour. Add in your sweetener, coconut oil, vanilla, salt, and flax egg, and process until everything is combined.
4. Pour the mixture into the prepared baking dish and bake for 22 minutes until the base becomes slightly golden and springs back when touched lightly.
5. Remove the baking dish from the oven (keep oven running though). Spread raspberry jam evenly over the top.

6. Sprinkle sliced almonds evenly on top of the jam. Return back to oven and bake for an additional 15 minutes until the almonds begin to get slightly golden.
7. Remove from oven and cool on a rack. Once cool, cut into squares and enjoy. I like these warm personally, but my husband likes chilled desserts better, so if you're that kind of person then just refrigerate for an hour or two to chill.

Peanut Butter And Banana S'mores

- SERVES 1

Ingredients
- 2 Peanut Butter and Banana Cookies (Gluten-Free)
- 1 tbsp Smooth Peanut Butter
- 1/8 tsp Molasses
- 6 Mini Marshmallows
- 10 – 15 Semi-Sweet Chocolate Chips

Directions
1. Turn oven on broil.
2. Stir together the peanut butter and molasses. It should thicken and firm up to a soft fudgy texture, if it doesn't, add a little more molasses.
3. Spread bottoms of both cookies with peanut butter mixture.
4. On one cookie arrange marshmallows on top of peanut butter, and on the other cookie sprinkle the chocolate chips over peanut butter.
5. Place both halves filling side up on a cookie sheet and broil until marshmallows brown (1 – 2 minutes). Watch them carefully, so they don't burn.
6. Gently lift cookies off sheet (they will be soft and may break apart easily) and sandwich them together.
7. Allow to cool for a few minutes before serving/devouring.

Vegan Tiramisu

Prep Time: 30 mins
Cook/CHill: Time 4 hours
Ready In: 4 hours 30 mins
Ingredients
"Ladyfingers" Layer Ingredients:
- 3 cup walnuts (not soaked)
- 2 cups medjool dates, pre-soaked (see notes above)
- ¼ cup strong coffee
- ⅛ tsp raw ground vanilla bean
- pinch of salt

Chocolate Mousse Layer Ingredients:
- 1½ - 2 cups medjool dates, pre-soaked
- Cream from 2 cans of full fat coconut milk:Note: for a raw version, use 1½ cups raw coconut cream
- 1½ cups walnuts, pre-soaked
- ½ cup very strong coffee
- ¼ cup coconut oil, melted
- ¼ cup cocoa powder {use raw cacao powder for raw version}
- ½ tsp raw ground vanilla
- pinch of salt
- ½ cup coconut water
- 2 tbsp agar agar flakes

Vanilla Cream Layer Ingredients:
- 1 cup cashews, pre-soaked (see notes above)
- ¼ cup coconut oil
- ½ cup coconut water or water (I used reserved coconut water from one of the cans in the previous step).
- 5 tbsp maple syrup

- ⅛ tsp raw ground vanilla bean

Topping:
- A bit of extra cocoa/raw cacao powder for dusting

Directions
1. Place walnuts in a food processor and process until mixture is fine and crumbly. Add in all remaining "ladyfingers" layer ingredients and process until the mixture is more or less smooth.
2. Transfer contents into a 9" springform pan and press base layer down evenly. Place the pan in the freezer while working on the next step.
3. Place all chocolate mousse layer ingredients, except for coconut water and agar-agar in your blender and blend until mixture is smooth
4. Set aside.
5. Place coconut water and agar agar in a small saucepan and warm on medium-low heat until the agar-agar flakes are dissolved, stirring occasionally.
6. Do not overcook, and do not allow the mixture to come to a boil.
7. Heat until the flakes just dissolve. Add this agar-agar mixture to the blender with the chocolate mousse ingredients and blend through to incorporate the two mixtures together.
8. Pour into the springform pan over the base layer and place back in the freezer for about an hour to chill and harden.
9. Prepare the vanilla cream layer by placing all the ingredients into a clean blender and blend until the mixture is smooth.
10. Set aside at room temperature. Once the chocolate mousse layer has been chilled for about an hour, pour the vanilla cream layer into the pan over the chocolate mousse.
11. Return cake to the freezer for at least 2-3 more hours.
12. Once the cake has chilled in the freezer for a total of 4 hours, remove the side of the pan and transfer cake onto a

serving plate. Dust the cake with some cocoa powder. I used some cacao nibs as well for garnish.
13. Now that the cake is ready, transfer it into the fridge and keep it refrigerated. You can serve right away as a chilled cake, but it's much more amazing after thawing out a little in the fridge as it actually becomes mousse-like. Alternatively, you can keep it frozen for longer storage.

Pumpkin Ice Cream And Brownie Parfait

Ingredients

For the ice cream

- 1 can organic pumpkin
- 1 can organic coconut milk
- 1/2 cup organic maple syrup
- 1 teaspoon organic vanilla extract
- 5 organic cloves
- 1 1/4 teaspoon organic nutmeg
- 2 teaspoons organic ginger

For the brownie

- 1/2 cup organic peanut butter
- 2/3 cups organic maple syrup
- 1/4 cup organic raw cacao powder
- 1/4 teaspoon pink himalayan salt
- 1/2 teaspoon baking soda
- 1 flax egg (1 tablespoon ground flax + 2 tablespoons water)

Direction

1. Prepare the ice cream
2. Put all ingredients for the ice cream into a Vitamix and blend until smooth and creamy.
3. Pour into your ice cream maker and prepare according to your ice cream makers instructions.
4. Prepare the brownies
5. Put all ingredients into a medium sized bowl and stir until well combined.
6. Pour into a glass baking dish and bake at 350 degrees for approximately 15 – 20 minutes or fully baked.
7. Let the brownies cool completely before adding to the parfait.
8. Assembly.

9. Take a piece of brownie and crumble into your bowl/dish as the bottom layer.
10. Add a couple of scoops of ice cream on top of the brownie.
11. Add another layer of brownie.
12. Add another layer of ice cream.

Pumpkin Mousse Tarts

Ingredients
Chocolate Shortbread Crust
- 1/4 cup (60 ml) coconut oil, solid at room temperature
- 1/4 cup (40 g) brown rice flour
- 1/3 cup (55 g) sorghum flour
- 2 Tbsp (15 ml) unsweetened cocoa powder
- 1/4 tsp (1 ml) xanthan gum, optional
- 1 Tbsp (15 ml) coconut (palm) sugar
- 1/4 tsp (1 ml) baking powder
- Pinch fine sea salt
- 2 Tbsp (30 ml) agave nectar or maple syrup
- 10-12 drops stevia liquid

Pumpkin Mousse Filling
- 1/4 cup (60 ml) plain or vanilla rice milk
- 2 Tbsp (30 ml) organic corn starch or tapioca starch
- 1 can (400 ml) full fat coconut milk (I use Thai Kitchen)
- 3/4 cup (180 ml) packed pumpkin puree (not pie filling)
- 1 tsp cinnamon
- 1/2 tsp ginger
- 1/4 tsp cloves
- 1/8 tsp nutmeg
- 1/8 tsp cardamom
- 2-1/4 tsp agar powder*

Chocolate Ganache
- 1 ounce (35 g) unsweetened chocolate, chopped
- 1 Tbsp (15 ml) agave nectar or maple syrup

Chocolate Shortbread Crust

1. Preheat oven to 350F (180C). Line 5 individual tart tins with parchment or spray with nonstick spray. Place the tart tins on a cookie sheet.
2. In the bowl of a food processor, combine the coconut oil, flours, cocoa, xanthan gum, palm sugar, baking powder and salt until evenly mixed and the coconut oil has broken up completely. Add the agave and stevia and whir again until a dough is formed (it may be a bit soft; this is fine).
3. Divide dough into 5 equal portions and press evenly into the tart tins. If necessary, wet your fingers to prevent sticking. Prick the bottom of each tart 2-3 times with a fork.
4. Bake in preheated oven until dry and beginning to brown on the edges, 20-25 minutes. Remove from oven and cool completely.

Pumpkin Mousse Filling
1. In a medium pot, blend the rice milk and starch until no lumps are visible.
2. Add the pumpkin and whisk until smooth, then add remaining ingredients and whisk again.
3. Cook over medium heat, stirring constantly, until the mixture begins to bubble; allow to bubble for 30 seconds. Remove from heat and cool to room temperature, stirring once after 5 minutes.
4. Refrigerate until cold (the mixture will be solid).
5. Break up the jelled mousse and place in a food processor, then process until smooth. Keep refrigerated until ready to serve.

Chocolate Ganache
1. Melt the chocolate and agave together in a small pot over lowest heat possible, stirring constantly, until melted. Drizzle over assembled tarts.

To assemble: spoon or pipe the pumpkin mousse filling into the cool tart shells, then drizzle with the chocolate ganache. Makes 5-6 small tarts. Store, covered, in the refrigerator, up to 3 days.

Chocolate Hazelnut Cheesecake

Ingredients
Crust
- 1 cup hazelnut meal
- 1/4 cup + 2 Tbsp raw cocoa powder
- 3 Tbsp maple syrup
- 1 tsp vanilla
- 1 pinch sea salt

Filling
- 2 cups raw cashews, soaked overnight and rinsed
- 1/4 cup + 2 Tbsp hazelnut butter (peanut butter works too)
- 1/2 cup coconut oil, melted
- 1/2 cup maple syrup
- 1/2 cup cocoa powder
- 1/2 cup water
- 1/2 tsp salt

Chocolate Sauce
- 1/3 cup coconut oil, melted
- 1 tsp vanilla
- 1/4 cup maple syrup
- 1/4 cup cocoa powder

Directions
1. The best pan to use for this recipe would be a Flexi-pan or other type of silicone mold. Otherwise a spring form pan works great. If you don't have a Flexi-pan but want individual cheesecakes, use a muffin pan, lightly oiled.
2. Blend all ingredients for the crust together in a food processor until it comes together. Remove from processor and press the crust into the bottom of desired pan, about 1/4 inch thick.

3. Set aside while you making the filling.
4. In a food processor or mixer blend together cashews, maple syrup, water, and salt. Run until totally smooth, scraping down the sides of the processor as necessary. Add cocoa powder, hazelnut butter and coconut oil to cashew mixture and blend together, scraping down again, until mixture is uniformly combine.
5. Spoon or pipe the filling on top of crusts. Stick cheesecake in the freezer until solid all the way through (at least 2 hours for individual cheesecakes, 4 for large cheesecake).
6. Once frozen remove cheesecake from pan. If using silicone mold, they will easily pop out. If you have a muffin tin, run a sharp, hot knife around the edges of each cheesecake. Using the knife as a lever, pop the cheesecakes out. If they don't come out easily, turn muffin tin upside down and give it a few whacks. Place the removed cakes in the refrigerator while making the chocolate sauce.
7. Mix the sauce ingredients together with a fork. Scoop a little onto cold cheesecake. Place back in fridge and let sauce harden.
8. Top with hazelnuts. Serve cold

Chocolate Pumpkin Tart

Crust Ingredients:
- 3 tbsp coconut oil, melted
- 3 tbsp maple syrup (or liquid sweetener of your choice), at room temperature
- 1/2 tbsp pure vanilla extract
- 7 tbsp pumpkin puree at room temp
- dash of salt
- 1/2 tsp cinnamon
- 1/2 cup coconut flour
- 3 tbsp tapioca flour

Filling Ingredients:
- 1 1/4 cup pumpkin puree (room temp)
- 1 cup coconut oil, very soft or liquified (but not hot)
- 1/2 cup cocoa powder
- 6 tbsp maple syrup (or liquid sweetener of your choice)
- 2 tsp pure vanilla extract
- pinch of salt
- 1 tsp cinnamon
- 1/8 tsp of each: cloves, allspice, and nutmeg

Spiderweb Ingredients:
- 2-3 tbsp non-dairy milk (I used almond)
- 1 1/2 tbsp coconut oil, liquified
- 2 tbsp coconut butter, warmed until liquified
- 1/2 tbsp maple syrup
- 1/2 tbsp tapioca starch

Directions:
1. Pre-heat oven to 350F. Oil your tart pan and set aside.
2. Place coconut oil, maple syrup, vanilla, pumpkin puree, salt, and cinnamon in a medium mixing bowl and use an

immersion blender to blend the mixture into a smooth consistency

3. If you don't have an immersion blender, blend all the ingredients in a regular blender and then pour into a mixing bowl.
4. Add coconut and tapioca flours and mix well using a wooden spoon until everything is thoroughly combined.
5. Scoop out the mixture into the pan. Use your hands to press the mixture down along the bottom and up around the walls of the pan forming the crust.
6. Use a fork to pierce some holes along the base of the crust to prevent bubbling during baking.
7. Bake in a pre-heated oven for 20 minutes. Remove from oven and allow the crust to cool in the pan on a wire rack for at least 10 minutes.

8. In the meantime, place all chocolate filling ingredients into a high-speed blender and process until mixture is smooth.
9. Once the tart shell has cooled, pour this mixture into the tart and smooth out the top with a spatula.
10. Blend the spiderweb mixture ingredients together until fully smooth. Note: start with just 2 tbsp milk and increase the quantity only if necessary so that the mixture is runny but not too thin.
11. Pour the spiderweb mixture into a squirty-bottle or piping bag and pour onto the top of the tart in a spiral pattern, starting in the center of the tart and drawing the spiral rings out until you reach the edges.
12. Then use a wooden skewer (or something similar), and gently draw a line from the center of the tart to the outer edge. Repeat this going all around the tart until you've created a spiderweb.

Mocha Ice Cream Sandwiches

Ingredients

Mocha Ice Cream
- 2 cans full fat coconut milk
- 1/4 cup cocoa powder
- 3 tsp instant espresso powder
- 1 cup organic granulated sugar
- 1/2 tsp salt

Mocha Cookie
- 3/4 cups vegan margarine
- 1 3/4 cups organic granulated sugar
- 1 tsp vanilla extract
- 2 tbsp flaxseed meal mixed with 4 tbsp water
- 1/2 tsp sea salt
- 1/2 cup + 2 tbsp cocoa powder
- 1 1/2 cups brown rice flour
- 1 cup sorghum flour
- 1/2 cup potato starch
- 1 tsp xanthan gum
- 2 tsp instant espresso powder

Directions

Mocha Ice Cream
1. Whisk together all ingredients vigorously until sugar has completely dissolved (warm mixture gently in a small pan over low heat if necessary to get all sugar granules to disappear).
2. Let mixture chill in fridge until all ingredients are cold.
3. Place mixture into ice cream maker and process according to manufacturer's instructions.

4. Don't let the ice cream freeze too long after it has finished in the ice cream maker, as you want the ice cream to be semi-soft for assembling your sandwiches.

Mocha Cookie
1. Preheat oven to 350 ºF.
2. Cream together margarine, sugar and vanilla extract until smooth.
3. Add in prepared flaxseed meal and mix well.
4. In separate mixing bowl, sift together salt, cocoa powder, brown rice flour, sorghum flour, potato starch, xanthan gum and espresso powder.
5. Gradually mix in dry ingredients with wet ingredients until all is very well combined. Continue mixing until dough clumps together.
6. Form into two disks and chill until very cold, about two hours in fridge, or thirty minutes in your freezer.
7. Once dough has thoroughly chilled, roll out one disk (using a lightly floured rolling pin) so that the dough is about 1/3 of an inch thick.
8. Use the top of a glass, or a round cookie cutter to cut out circle shapes.
9. Place about 2" apart onto ungreased cookie sheet and bake 9-11 minutes.
10. Remove from oven and do not disturb the cookies until they are fully cooled.
11. Repeat with the rest of your dough until all has been rolled, cut out and baked.

Assemble your sandwiches
1. Chill baked cookies in fridge briefly until cold (if they are even slightly warm, they will cause the ice cream to melt!), and then pile ice cream (about 1/3 cup) onto one cookie and squish down gently with another cookie to make a sandwich.
2. Freeze about 2 hours or until sandwich firms up.

Maple Nut Cake
- Serves 1/6 inch 4 layer cake

Salted Maple Nuts:
- 1 cup sliced almonds
- 1 cup sliced walnuts
- 2 Tbsp maple syrup
- 2 Tbsp maple sugar
- 1/2 tsp sea salt

Cake:
- 1/2 cup almond flour
- 1/4 cup ground hazelnut meal
- 1/4 cup ground walnut meal*
- 3/4 cup coconut flour
- 1 1/2 tsp baking soda
- 1 tsp sea salt
- 1 cup maple sugar or granulated sugar
- 1/2 cup coconut oil
- 1 1/2 cups lite organic coconut milk or almond milk
- 1 Tbsp pure vanilla extract
- 2 tsp maple extract
- 2 Tbsp cider vinegar

Frosting:
- 2 8 oz pkgs tofutti vegan cream cheese
- 1/2 cup almond butter
- 1/2 cup plus 2 Tbsp maple syrup
- 1 Tbsp pure vanilla extract
- 2 tsp maple extract
- a pinch of sea salt

Directions

1. The Nuts – preheat the oven to 375 and place them on a sheet with foil. Utilize maple syrup, sugar, and salt to mix them together before toasting. 10 minute swill work here.

2. The Cake – You will need 2 round cake pans, that are at least 2 inches high. Line the sides with paper, and utilize nonstick spray so that you can take them out. Combine the ingredients together and make sure it's blended very well. Take the batter and put in the pans, baking for 30 minutes. Let them cool afterwards for no less than 1 hour.
3. The Frosting – Whip together vegan cream cheese, smoothing it out, add almond butter, vanilla, maple syrup, and the rest of the ingredients until it's 100% smooth.
4. Put the cake together layer by layer. You'll want to take your time spreading the frosting, and use time to smooth out all the elements together. Add the nuts for decoration, and that's it.
5. Adding more layers to this can work, just expand the frosting recipe to cover more.

Healthy Oreo Cake

- Prep Time: 5 minutes
- Cook Time: 25 minutes
- Yield: 9 in circle cake, if you double it makes two 9 in cakes
- serves 6 -8

Ingredients

- 1 green-yellow plantain (8oz weighed raw, about 1 1/3 cups plantain cut into large cubes)
- 1/2 cup applesauce (4 oz)
- 1/4 cup coconut oil, liquid (2 oz)
- 2 tablespoons coconut butter (1 1/4 oz)
- 1/2 teaspoon baking powder
- 1/2 teaspoon baking soda
- 1/2 teaspoon sea salt (optional)
- 4 tablespoons protein powder (1 oz)
- 2/3 cup raw cacao powder (2 1/2oz)

Directions

1. Preheat oven to 350 degrees.
2. Peel and chop up plantains.
3. Place 1/4 cup coconut oil, 2 tbsp coconut butter, 8 oz plantain and 1/2 cup applesauce into vitamix blender
4. Blend together.
5. Next add in 1/2 tsp baking powder, 1/2 tsp baking soda, 1/2 tsp sea salt, 4 tbsp protein powder and 2/3 cup cocoa powder.
6. Blend until everything is well blended and smooth.
7. Lightly grease a 9 in circle cake pan.
8. Pour cake batter into pan.
9. Set aside while you make the second layer.
10. Make second cake. Repeat the previous steps.

11. Pour into the second 9 in circle cake pan that has been greased.
12. Bake in oven for about 25 minutes.
13. Make frosting while cakes bake.
14. Let cool in pans before removing.
15. Carefully remove from pans.
16. Spread the frosting on one of the cakes.
17. Carefully top the second cake on top.

Chocolate Kale Brownies

- Prep time 15 mins
- Cook time 25 mins
- Total time 40 mins
- Serves: 12 to 16

Ingredients

- ¾ cup gluten-free flour (I used ½ cup brown rice, ¼ cup arrowroot)
- ½ cup cocoa powder
- ¾ cup coconut sugar
- ½ tsp baking powder
- ½ cup coconut milk (full fat)
- ¼ cup melted coconut oil
- ½ cup lightly packed shredded zucchini
- 1 cup finely shredded, lightly packed kale
- ½ tsp vanilla powder, or 1 tsp vanilla extract
- pinch of salt

Direction

1. Preheat the oven to 350 degress F.
2. In a medium-sized bowl, mix the flour, cocoa powder, coconut sugar, baking powder and salt. Add in the coconut milk, coconut oil and vanilla, and stir until everything is well mixed.
3. Fold in the kale and zucchini.
4. Lightly grease an 8x8-inch baking pan with coconut oil, then pour in the batter and smooth it out evenly.
5. Bake for 22 to 25 minutes, depending on how fudgy you like your brownies. Makes 12 to 16 squares.

Mini Crunch Bars With Peanut Butter Shell Drizzle

- 12 MINI BARS
- Freeze Time: 15MINUTES
- Prep TIme: 5 MINUTES

Ingredients:

Crunch Bar

- 1/2 cup coconut oil
- 1/2 cup unsweetened cocoa powder
- 5 tablespoons liquid sweetener (maple syrup, agave, etc.), or to taste
- pinch of fine grain sea salt, to taste
- 1 teaspoon pure vanilla extract
- 1 cup rice crisp cereal

Peanut Butter Shell Drizzle

- 2 tablespoons all-natural peanut butter
- 1.5-2 teaspoons coconut oil, as needed to thin out
- 1 teaspoon liquid sweetener (maple syrup, agave, etc.)

Directions:

1. For the crunch bar: Line a 9x5 inch loaf pan with two pieces of parchment paper, one going each way. In a pot over low heat, gently melt the coconut oil and then whisk in the rest of the crunch bar ingredients (except the rice crisp) to taste. Once the mixture is smooth remove from heat and stir in the rice crisp cereal. Pour mixture into prepared pan, smooth out, and then freeze for 10-15 minutes, or until the chocolate is solid.
2. For the PB drizzle: Melt the coconut oil and then whisk in the peanut butter and liquid sweetener. Adjust to taste if desired. Scoop into a plastic baggie.

3. Remove crunch bar from freezer and cut into 12 small bars. Snip a tiny hole in the baggie and drizzle the PB mixture onto the bar
4. Return bars to the freezer until the PB drizzle is solid, about 5 minutes.
5. Serve straight from the freezer or fridge. Bars will melt slightly at room temperature so I don't suggest keeping them out long. Store leftovers in the fridge or freezer.

Raw Coconut Snowballs

- Prep Time: 10 mins
- Ready In: 10 mins
- Makes: 10 snowballs

INGREDIENTS

- 1 cup coconut butter
- 1 cup shredded coconut
- 3 tbsp maple syrup (or liquid sweetener of choice)
- 2 tsp pure vanilla extract (or a pinch of raw ground vanilla beans)
- ½ cup more shredded coconut for rolling (or can roll in some powdered sugar for a more "snowy" look)

Directions

1. Place all ingredients except the ½ cup shredded coconut into a food processor and process until everything is combined and the mixture begins to form a ball.
2. Spread the coconut reserved for rolling onto a plate and set aside.
3. Form bite sized balls out of the dough by shaping and rolling them with your hands, and then give them a roll on the shredded coconut plate to coat them.
4. Serve/eat right away or refrigerate for a little bit to make them firmer. They can be made ahead too and store well in the fridge or can be frozen.

Raw Spice Cookie Dough Bites

- 1 cup raw cashews
- 1/4 cup warm water
- 7 large Medjool dates, pitted - lightly soaked in hot water
- 1/2 banana
- 2-3 Tbsp organic virgin coconut oil, cold-pressed/raw - softened or melted
- 1/4 tsp cinnamon
- 1/4 tsp real vanilla extract or 1 vanilla bean (pod scraped of seeds)
- 1/4 tsp orange or lemon zest
- 1/8 tsp salt
- dash of cayenne (optional)
- 1-2 tsp maca powder (optional)

Spiced Cacao Raw Cookie Dough Bites

- Serves 20 balls or 10 bars

Ingredients

- 1 cup raw almonds
- 2-3 Tbsp warm water
- 10 large Medjool dates, pitted - lightly soaked in hot water
- 1 Tbsp organic virgin coconut oil, cold-pressed/raw - softened or melted
- 2 Tbsp raw organic cacao powder
- 1/4 tsp cinnamon
- 1/8 tsp salt
- 1/4 tsp real vanilla extract or 1 vanilla bean
- dash of cayenne (optional)
- 1-2 tsp maca powder (optional)

Directions

Tools: Powerful Food Processor

1. The coconut oil is what helps these balls firm up when chilled, so don't be afraid of adding more oil if you want them more rich and decadent
2. If desired, omit the oil or you will be left with a very soft paste that never fully chills/hardens.
3. Pit your dates and soak them in some warm water for 1-2 minutes.
4. Melt or soften coconut oil. Add the nuts to your appliance and grind until fine to slightly chunky
5. Next add in the remaining ingredients and process until smooth yet chunky.
6. For bars: Oil your freezing container with coconut oil. Place in freezer until firm enough to slice. Serve or store on parchment paper. Add chocolate drizzle to cold bars if desired - the chocolate drizzle will firm up quickly upon contact with the cold bar.

7. For balls: Freeze until cool and firm enough to handle. Using your hands or a cookie dough scooper, mold into balls. Add vegan chocolate chips on top and line up on a plate. Freeze until you are ready to enjoy.
8. Serve straight from freezer or warm at room temperature for a few minutes to soften. Store in fridge or freezer.

Deep Dish Cookie Pie

- 2 cans white beans or garbanzos (drained and rinsed) (500g total, once drained)
- 1 cup quick oats (or certified-gf quick oats)
- 1/4 cup unsweetened applesauce
- 3 tbsp oil (canola, veg, or coconut)
- 2 tsp pure vanilla extract
- 1/2 tsp baking soda
- 2 tsp baking powder
- 1/2 tsp salt
- 1 and 1/2 cups brown sugar
- 1 cup chocolate chips

Directions
1. Blend everything (except the chips) very well in a good food processor
2. Mix in chips, and pour into an oiled pan
3. Cook at 350F for around 35-40 minutes.
4. Let stand at least 10 minutes before removing from the pan.

Apricot & Salt Chocolate Tart

- Serves 8-12

Hazelnut Crust
- 1 1/2 cups toasted hazelnuts
- 1 1/4 cups almond meal
- 2 tbl organic light brown sugar
- pinch of sea salt
- 1/2 cup melted coconut oil

Directions
1. Preheat the oven to 350.
2. In a food processor, blend the hazelnuts, almond meal, brown sugar and salt in a food processor until the hazelnuts have been ground into fine crumbs.
3. Add the oil and pulse a few times more until the crust starts to come together.
4. Press the nut mixture firmly into a 9" spring form tart pan.
5. Bake for 15 minutes until lightly golden. Set aside to cool.

Apricot Chocolate Filling

Ingredients
- 8 oz bittersweet chocolate, roughly chopped
- 8 oz semisweet chocolate, roughly chopped, divided
- 3 tbl organic cane sugar
- 2 tbl coconut oil
- 1/4 tsp fine sea salt
- 1 cup apricot nectar
- 8-12 dried apricots

Directions
1. Combine the bittersweet chocolate with 4 ounces semisweet chocolate, sugar, coconut oil and salt.
2. Bring the nectar to a boil and pour over the chocolate.
3. Whisk until the ganache is smooth.
4. Pour into the cooled tart shell and chill until the filling is solid.
5. Melt the remaining 4 ounces of semisweet chocolate and dip the dried apricots for garnish.

Rocky Road Fudge

- 3 cups sugar
- 3/4 cup Earth Balance
- 2/3 cup full fat coconut milk
- 12 oz semisweet chocolate
- 1 bag Dandies, halved
- 1/2 cup Ricemellow Creme
- 2 tsp vanilla
- 1/2 cup chopped almonds

1. Line a 9" square pan with parchment.
2. Chop almonds and half of the dandies into small 1/4" pieces.
3. In a heavy bottomed, large pan combine the sugar, Earth Balance, and coconut milk.
4. Stir continuously over medium heat until it comes to a rolling boil.
5. Allow to boil for 5 minutes.
6. Stir in chocolate, vanilla, Ricemellow creme, and the uncut Dandies. You will need to stir quickly.(recommend an electric mixer)
7. Fold in almonds and remaining marshmallows and pour into the pan.
8. Allow to cool for at least 2 hours before slicing into squares with a sharp knife.

Black Bean Apple Brownies

Ingredients
- 1 c black beans
- 1 apple
- 2 Tbsp flaxseeds
- 3 Tbsp warm water
- 2 Tbsp cashew milk
- 1 Tbsp shortening
- 1/2 tsp vanilla
- 1/4 c agave
- 1/8 tsp salt
- 1 tsp baking powder
- 1/4 c coconut flour
- 1/4 c cocoa powder
- 2 tsp millet flour
- 1/3 c vegan chocolate chips
- Shortening

Directions:

1. Preheat oven to 350 degrees fahrenheit, 335 convection.

2. Grind flax seeds in a spice grinder or small blender, like a Magic Bullet.

3. Add warm water, stir, then let sit for at least 3 minutes.

4. Drain a can of black beans, then rinse.

5. Measure about a cup of the beans and put them in a food processor.

6. Peel and core an apple, then shop it into small pieces. Add to food processor then pulse mixture until smooth, scraping down the sides occasionally.

7. Add remaining liquid ingredients. Pulse, then add dry ingredients, and pulse again.

8. Remove food processor blade, then add vegan chocolate chips. Gently mix.

9. Transfer batter into a pan greased with vegetable shortening. Bake for about 20 minutes.

10. Let cool for another 20 minutes.

Chocolate Pots De Crème

- Prep Time: 15 minutes
- Total Time: 3 hours, 15 minutes
- Yield: 2 large or 3 small pots

Ingredients

- 1 14 oz can regular coconut milk
- 5 oz bittersweet chocolate, coarsely chopped
- 1/2 cup basil leaves, coarsely torn (I used about 1/4 cup)
- 2 Tablespoons agave nectar
- 1 teaspoon orange zest
- 1/2 teaspoon vanilla extract
- 1/4 teaspoon crushed peppercorns (I just used a few turns of black pepper from the pepper grinder)

Directions:

1. Put the coconut milk in a small pot over medium heat and bring to a simmer.
2. Put the chocolate in a blender or food processor and pour the hot coconut milk over it. Add basil, agave, orange zest, vanilla extract, and pepper and blend until chocolate is melted and mixture is smooth.
3. Strain through a fine-mesh sieve (I skipped this step but did have small flecks of basil in the final dish so you may want to strain yours to make it super smooth.) Divide among four small cups. Cover and refrigerate until set, about 3 hours.

Blueberry Lime Cheesecake

- Prep Time: 20 mins
- Total Time: 20 mins

Ingredients

- 4 Medjool Dates
- 1 cup Macadamia Nuts (raw, unsalted)
- Pinch of Salt
- 2 cups Coconut Cream (see notes)
- ⅔ of a cup Cashews (soaked in water for 10-15 minutes)
- 4 tablespoons Fresh Lime Juice
- 2 tablespoons Maple Syrup
- 2 Medjool Dates
- 1 cup fresh Blueberries
- 1 teaspoon Lime Zest (optional)
- ½ cup fresh Blueberries (optional)

Directions

1. Line a 7 inch springform with parchment paper.
2. Place macadamia nuts, 4 dates and pinch of salt in food processor and pulse until a sticky mass forms.
3. Press macadamia crust into bottom of springform and half way up the sides using fingers. place in freezer while you prepare the filling.
4. Clean out food processor and place coconut cream, cashews, lime juice, and maple syrup in it. Pulse and process until mixture is smooth.
5. Remove springform from freezer and pour lemon cheesecake filling into the springform. Place springform in freezer again until filling in slightly firm (about 10 minutes).
6. Clean out food processor again and place blueberries and 2 dates in it. Pulse again until smooth (blueberry skin will still

be present, this is OK). Carefully spread blueberry topping over filling in the springform.
7. Place in refrigerator for at least 4 hours or overnight until filling is firm.
8. When cheesecake is firm and ready to serve garnish with fresh blueberries and lime zest.

NOTES
- Cashews can be soaked in water for 10-15 minutes first to make filling extra smooth. Make sure to dry off excess water from them before placing them in food processor.
- The cheesecake recipe calls for 2 cups Coconut cream. This can be store bought coconut cream. Alternatively, you can place 2 cans of coconut milk in the refrigerator for at least 2 hours, then scoop the thick creamy part out of the can. Depending on the coconut milk brand, either 1 or 2 cans of coconut milk will yield 2 cups coconut cream.
- Blueberry lime cheesecake can also be placed in the freezer to help firm the filling up quickly. I find that it takes a long time for it to thaw to the point of the cheesecake being nice and smooth. However, if you are planning on transporting the cheesecake then having it frozen works wonders.
- Cheesecake will keep in refrigerator for up to 4 days.
- Crust can easily be made with other nuts as well. Almonds, hazelnuts, and walnuts work well.

Pumpkin Pie

- Prep time: 1 hour
- Cook time: 1 hour
- Total time: 2 hours

Ingredients

CRUST

- 6 Tbsp cold vegan butter (or chilled coconut oil with varied results)
- 1 1/4 cup Bob's Red Mill 1:1 Gluten Free Flour
- 1/4 tsp salt
- 4-6 Tbsp ice cold water

FILLING

- 2 3/4 cups pumpkin puree
- 1/4 cup maple syrup
- 1/4 cup brown sugar
- 1/3 cup unsweetened plain almond milk
- 1 Tbsp olive oil, or melted coconut oil
- 2 1/2 Tbsp cornstarch or arrowroot powder
- 1 3/4 tsp pumpkin pie spice (or sub mix of ginger, cinnamon, nutmeg & cloves)
- 1/4 tsp sea salt

Directions

1. To prepare crust, add gluten free flour and salt to a large mixing bowl and whisk to combine. Slice or dollop the cold butter in and work gently with a fork or pastry cutter to cut it in.
2. Next add ice cold water a little at a time and use a wooden spoon to stir. Only add as much water as you need to help it come together.

3. Once a loose dough is formed, transfer to a piece of plastic wrap and work gently with your hands to form a 1/2 inch thick disc. Wrap firmly and refrigerate for a 1-2 hours.
4. Once your dough is chilled, preheat oven to 350 degrees F and prepare pie filling.
5. Add all pie ingredients to a blender and blend until smooth, scraping down sides as needed. Taste and adjust seasonings as needed. Set aside.
6. To roll out the crust, unwrap the disc and place it between two sizable layers of wax paper (plastic wrap will work OK, but is a little more difficult to work with). Use a rolling pin to gently roll it into the shape of your pie pan.
7. To transfer the crust, remove the top layer of wax paper and gently lay the pie dish face down on top of the crust and use the support of the wax paper to quickly but carefully invert it.
8. Once you get the crust inverted, gently use your hands to form it into the pan, working the crust up along the sides.
9. Any holes or cracks can be mended with a little excess dough and the heat of your hand.
10. TIP: I would advise against trying to be fancy and do any elaborate design with the crust, so just get the crust in, get a flat edge and go.
11. Pour filling into pie crust and bake at 350 for 58-65 minutes. The crust should be light golden brown and the filling will still be just a bit jiggly and have some cracks on the top. Remove from oven and let cool completely before loosely covering and transferring to the refrigerator to fully set for 4-6 hours, preferably overnight.
12. Slice and serve with coconut whipped cream and an additional sprinkle of cinnamon, nutmeg, and/or pumpkin pie spice

Blueberry, Lemon, Poppy Seed & Almond Cake

- Serves 8-10

Ingredients
- 4 cups (400 g) almond flour
- 3 tbsp poppy seeds
- 1/2 tsp salt
- 1 tsp baking powder
- 1/2 tsp baking soda
- 1/2 cup (120 ml) rapeseed oil or ghee
- 1/2 cup (120 ml) honey or maple syrup
- 2 small organic lemons
- 3 large eggs (replace with chia seeds* if you are vegan)
- 2 cups (300 g) blueberries (save half for topping)
- Glazing
- 1 cup/240 ml (250 g) Turkish yogurt, drained (use vegan cream cheese if you are vegan)
- 2 tbsp honey or maple syrup
- 1 tsp vanilla extract

Directions
1. Preheat oven to 350°F / 180°C.
2. Combine almond flour, poppy seeds, salt, baking powder and baking soda in a large bowl and set aside.
3. Heat oil and honey in a sauce pan on very low heat until combined. Grate the zest from the 2 lemons and add it to the honey/oil batter.
4. Divide them in half and squeeze the juice from three of the halves into the mixture, saving one half for the glazing.
5. Add the batter to the bowl with the dry ingredients.
6. Beat the eggs and then fold them into the batter together with 1 cup of the blueberries.

7. Stir gently around with a wooden spoon until combined. Grease a 8-inch spring form cake tin, and add the batter to it.
8. Bake for about 40-50 minutes (depending on size of the pan and oven), or until golden on the outside and baked all way through (you can cover the cake with tin foil during the last 15 minutes of the baking time, if it starts looking burned) .
9. Remove from oven and let cool for at least 30 minutes before removing the sides. Meanwhile, start making the glazing.
10. Drain yogurt in a milk cloth or coffee filter for about 10 minutes. This is to make the yogurt less runny.
11. Discard the water and combine the thick yogurt with honey vanilla extract and the juice from the remaining lemon half.
12. Leave to chill in the fridge. When the cake has cooled completely, cover it with glazing, top with the remaining blueberries and serve.
13. You could also just serve the cake with blueberries and yogurt on the side.

Blueberry Crisp Tart With Oat Crust

Ingredients

For the filling
- 1 pint (300 grams or about 2 cups) fresh blueberries
- 1 tablespoon honey (or maple syrup to keep vegan)
- 2 teaspoons tapioca starch

For the crust
- 1 cup (4 oz) almond flour
- ¾ cup (2½ oz) old-fashioned oats
- ¼ cup (3 oz) honey (or maple syrup to keep vegan)
- 1 teaspoon baking powder
- ½ teaspoon salt
- 5 tablespoons coconut oil, solid
- 2 tablespoons chopped pecans

Directions
1. Preheat the oven to 350 degrees F.
2. Add blueberries, honey or maple syrup, and tapioca starch to a medium bowl and toss until coated. Set the blueberries aside while you make the crust.
3. Add the almond flour, oats, honey or maple syrup, baking powder, and salt to a different bowl and whisk until combined. Add the coconut oil and use your fingers to work it in until coarse crumbs form and the mixture holds together when pressed.
4. Remove a heaping ½ cup of the crumbs for the topping and pour the remaining crumbs into the bottom of a 9-inch tart pan with a removable bottom. Press the dough evenly into the pan. Pour the blueberries over the crust, making sure the juices stay behind in the bottom of the bowl.
5. Add the chopped pecans to the remaining crumble and sprinkle evenly over the top of the berries.

6. Bake for 40-45 minutes or until the filling is bubbling and the crust is lightly brown. At around 20 minutes, tent the tart with foil to prevent it from getting too brown.
7. Let cool completely before slicing into wedges and serving.

Summer Berry Crisps

- Makes 4 servings

Ingredients

Crisp Topping:
- ½ C. gluten-free flour
- 1 t. ground cardamom
- ½ C. sugar
- ¾ C. combination of chopped pumpkin seeds and sunflower seeds
- ¾ C. ground Flax Original Cereal
- ⅓ C. shortening

Berry Filling:
- 18 oz. mixed berries, fresh or frozen
- 1 t. tapioca starch
- 1 T. fresh lemon juice
- ¼ C. sugar

Directions
1. Preheat oven to 350°.
2. Line a rimmed baking sheet with parchment paper and place 4- 1-cup ramekins on top. Set aside.
3. Put all the ingredients for the topping in a bowl and mix together with a pastry blender, a fork, or your hands. Mix until the shortening is evenly mixed through and the mixture feels a little sandy.
4. In another small bowl mix together the berry filling, gently tossing until everything is coated with the sugar.
5. Pour the berry mixture evenly into the 4 ramekins and top with ¼ C. of the crisp topping.
6. Bake for 30-35 minutes until the berry juices are bubbling and the crisp is just lightly browned on top.

7. Cool 10 minutes and then serve while warm!

Dark Chocolate Cereal Cookies

- Makes 18 cookies

Ingredients
- 1 ½ C. Dark Chocolate Morsels
- ¼ C. sunflower seed butter
- 2 T. chia seeds
- 1 ½ C. Flax Cereal

Directions
1. Melt together the Dark Chocolate Morsels and sunflower seed butter until smooth.
2. Add the chia seeds and the Perky's Crunchy Cereal and stir until combined and the cereal is completely coated in chocolate.
3. Drop by tablespoon on a parchment lined sheet tray and place in the fridge to set.
4. Store in a container in the fridge for 7-10 days.

Chocolate Cereal Cookies

- Makes 18 cookies

Ingredients
- 1 ½ C. Enjoy Life Foods Dark Chocolate Morsels
- ¼ C. sunflower seed butter
- 2 T. chia seeds
- 1 ½ C. Enjoy Life Foods Perky's Crunchy Flax Cereal (or Chia!)

Directions
1. Melt together the Dark Chocolate Morsels and sunflower seed butter until smooth.
2. Add the chia seeds and the Perky's Crunchy Cereal and stir until combined and the cereal is completely coated in chocolate.
3. Drop by tablespoon on a parchment lined sheet tray and place in the fridge to set.
4. Store in a container in the fridge for 7-10 days.

Boomin Style Onion Rings

- 4 cups canola oil
- 4.4 ounces gluten-free all-purpose flour
- 5 ounces white rice flour
- 1 tablespoon chili powder
- 1 teaspoon baking soda
- 1 1/4 cups club soda, chilled
- 1 medium onion, cut into 1/2-inch-thick slices and separated into rings (8 ounces)
- 1/4 teaspoon salt
- 1/4 teaspoon garlic powder
- 1/4 teaspoon black pepper
- 1/2 cup ketchup (optional)

Directions
1. Preheat oven to 200°.
2. Clip a candy thermometer onto the side of a 4-quart Dutch oven; add oil to pan. Heat oil to 385°.
3. While oil heats, weigh or lightly spoon flours into dry measuring cups; level with a knife. Combine flours, chili powder, and baking soda in a medium bowl. Gradually add club soda, stirring with a whisk until smooth.
4. Dip onion rings, 1 at a time, in batter, coating completely.
5. Add to hot oil. (Do not crowd pan.) Fry 1 minute on each side or until golden, maintaining temperature of oil at 375°.
6. Drain onion rings on a paper towel–lined jelly-roll pan.
7. Place pan in oven and keep warm at 200° until ready to serve. Combine salt, garlic powder, and black pepper.
8. Sprinkle onion rings evenly with salt mixture just before serving. Serve with ketchup, if desired.

Arugula And Cremini Quiche With Gluten-Free Almond Meal Crust

Ingredients
Almond meal crust
- 2 cups almond meal or almond flour (I had better results with almond meal)
- 3 garlic cloves, pressed or minced
- 1 tablespoon minced fresh thyme or 1 teaspoon dried thyme
- ½ teaspoon salt
- ¼ teaspoon freshly ground pepper
- ⅓ cup olive oil
- 1 tablespoon and 1 teaspoon water

Arugula, Cremini mushroom and goat cheese filling
- 3 cups baby arugula, roughly chopped
- 1½ cups cleaned and sliced Cremini mushrooms
- Drizzle olive oil
- 6 large eggs
- ⅓ cup milk
- ½ teaspoon salt
- ¼ teaspoon red pepper flakes
- 5 ounces goat cheese, crumbled

Directions

1. Preheat oven to 400 degrees Fahrenheit. Grease a 10-inch cast iron skillet or large tart pan with cooking spray. In a mixing bowl, stir together the almond meal, garlic, thyme, salt and pepper. Pour in the olive oil and water and stir until the mixture is thoroughly combined.
2. Press the dough into your prepared skillet/pan until it is evenly dispersed across the bottom and up the sides (if you are using a cast iron skillet, make sure the dough goes at

least 1¼ inch up the sides). Bake until the crust is lightly golden and firm to the touch, about 18 to 20 minutes.
3. In a large skillet over medium heat, warm enough olive oil to lightly coat the pan. Cook the mushrooms with a dash of salt, stirring often, until tender. Toss in the arugula and let it wilt, while stirring, about 30 seconds. Transfer the mixture to a plate to cool.
4. In a mixing bowl, whisk together the eggs, milk, salt and red pepper. Stir in the goat cheese and the slightly cooled mushroom and arugula mixture.
5. Once the crust is done baking, pour in the egg mixture and bake for 30 minutes, or until the center is firm to the touch and cooked through. Let the quiche cool for 5 to 10 minutes before slicing with a sharp knife. Serve immediately.

Gingerbread Dough/House

- Prep Time: 60 minute
- Serves: 36

Ingredients

Wet

- 1.5 cups vegetable shortening
- 1.5 cups of firmly packed brown sugar
- 1.5 cups unsulfured blackstrap molasses
- 1.5 teaspoon pure vanilla extract

Dry

- 3.75 teaspoon baking soda
- 3/4 teaspoon Himalayan rock salt
- 3 tablespoon freshly ground flax seed
- 1.5 cup teff flour
- 2.25 cup light buckwheat flour
- 1.5 cup sorghum flour
- 1.5 cup tapioca flour
- 3/4 cup chickpea flour
- 2.5 tablespoon ground ginger
- 1 tablespoon ground cinnamon
- 1.5 teaspoon ground nutmeg
- 3/4 teaspoon ground cloves

Candy

- Gluten-free candies like M&Ms, skittles, Mike n' ikes, Swedish berries, hard candies, jelly tots, or jube jubes

Ingredients
1. Preheat oven to 350F and line a couple of baking sheets with parchment paper or a silicon baking mat.
2. Combine shortening and brown sugar in a large bowl and mix with hand blender until light and fluffy. Add the molasses and vanilla and continue to mix. Set aside.
3. In a separate bowl, combine all dry ingredients and mix with a large spoon. Transfer to the wet mixture and beat with hand mixer until incorporated.
4. The dough will be crumbly at first but will come together and a couple of minutes. Finish kneading by hand.
5. The dough can be used right away, no need to chill. Take sections of the dough and roll out to about 1/4-inch thickness. If you don't want to use the do right away, wrap in plastic and store in the fridge overnight.
6. There is no need to flour the surface of your counter, the mix is very easy to work with!
7. Cut desired shapes and place on the prepared baking sheet.
8. Bake for 8-12 minutes, depending on the sizes of your cut outs. We found that the smaller pieces were good with 8 minutes, and the larger pieces were perfect at 12 minutes.
9. Remove from the oven and allow to cool on the baking sheet for 5 minutes before transferring to a cooling rack.

Cashew Beef

Ingredients:
- 1 Large Sized Red Onion – Quartered
- 4 Cloves of Garlic – Crushed
- 1 Inch Cube of Ginger – Peeled
- 2 tsp. of Ghee
- ¾ tsp. of Cumin – Ground
- ¾ tsp. of Coriander – Ground
- ½ tsp. of Cardamom - Ground
- ½ tsp. of Cloves – Ground
- ½ tsp. of Cinnamon
- ½ tsp. of Slat
- ½ tsp. of Pepper
- 1 Pound of Round Beef – Cut to Pieces
- 1 Cup of Frozen Peas
- 2/3 Cup of Low Fat Greek Yogurt
- 1/3 Cup of Toasted Cashews

Directions:
1. Combine the garlic, onion, and the ginger in a food processor. Puree it.
2. Melt the ghee in the pan on medium heat and then stir in the coriander, cumin, cardamom, cinnamon, cloves, salt, and the pepper.
3. Heat it and stir it constantly for 1-2 minutes.
4. Add in the onion and pulse it just a few times.
5. Combine the onion mix and the beef and cook it for a few minutes.
6. Add everything to the cooker except for the peas and the yogurt. Stir those in for last 15 minutes of the cook time.

7. Garnish it with the cashews.

Nutritional Information per serving:

Calories: 314 Total Fat: 14g Carb: 16g Protein: 32g

Ground Sirloin

Ingredients:

- 1 Pound of Ground Sirloin
- 1 Large Sized of Yellow Onion – Chopped
- 2 Cloves of Garlic – Minced
- 4 Large Sized Beets – Peeled, Chopped
- 4 Large Sized Carrots – Peeled, Chopped
- 2 Ribs of Celery – Chopped
- 2 Medium Potatoes – Un-Peeled, Chopped
- 1 Cup of Green Cabbage – Sliced Thin
- 6 Cups of Beef Broth
- ¼ Cup of Tomato Paste
- 2 tsp. of Beef Bouillon
- 1 tsp. of Carawy Seeds
- ½ tsp. of Salt
- ½ tsp. of Pepper
- 3 Tbsp. of Red Wine Vinegar
- ½ Cup of Greek Yogurt
- ¼ Cup of Dill – Fresh, Chopped

Directions:

1. In a large pan on medium high heat, combine the onion, sirloin, and the garlic. Cook it for 5-6 minutes until there is no pink.
2. Remove the heat and drain the liquid and put it in the cooker.
3. Add in the carrots, beets, celery, cabbage, potatoes, broth, tomato paste, caraway seeds, bouillon, salt, and the pepper.
4. Stir the mix very well. Cover it and allow it to cook 6-7 hours or until the vegetables are tender.

5. Stir in the vinegar during the last 10 minutes of the cooking time.
6. In a small mixing bowl, combine the yogurt and the dill. Store it in the refrigerator.
7. Serve the bowls with a drop of dilled yogurt on top.

Nutritional Information per serving:

Calories: 243 Total Fat: 5g Carbohydrates: 27g Protein: 24g

Sirloin Tip Chili

Ingredients:
- 2 Pounds of Sirloin Tip
- 1 tsp. of Sea Salt – Divided
- ½ tsp. of Pepper
- 2 ½ Tbsp. of Olive Oil – Divided
- 2 Large Sized Red Onions – Chopped
- 1 Large Sized Green Bell Pepper – Seeded, Chopped
- 1 Medium Sized Jalapeno Pepper – Seeded, Chopped Fine
- 6 Cloves of Garlic
- 3 Tbsp. of Chili Powder
- ¾ tsp. of Ancho Chile Pepper
- 1 ½ tsp. of Cumin – Ground
- 1 tsp. of Oregano – Dried
- 2 Cups of Beef Broth
- 1 ½ Cups of Corona Beer
- 14 ½ Ounces of Tomato Puree
- 14 ½ Ounces of Fire Roasted Tomatoes – Un-drained
- 1/3 Cup of Tomato Paste
- 1/3 Cup of Polenta – Dried
- 15 Ounces of White Kidney Beans – Drained, Rinsed
- 15 Ounce of Red Kidney Beans 0 Drained, Rinsed
- 1 tsp. of Sucanat
- ½ Cup of Scallions – Chopped
- ½ Cup of Cilantro – Fresh, Chopped

Directions:
1. Trim the visible fat off of the meat and cut it to bite sized pieces.

2. Season the meat with the salt and the pepper.
3. Heat 1 Tbsp. of oil in a large pan on medium high heat and brown it on all of the sides.
4. Transfer the meat to your slow cooker.
5. Reduce the heat to a medium heat and add in the 1 ½ Tbsp. of oil, bell pepper, onions, and the jalapeno pepper in to your pan and cook it for about 5 minutes.
6. Add in the garlic, chili pepper, chili powder, oregano, cumin, and then cook it for 1 minute stirring it continuously.
7. Transfer the ingredients from the pan to the cooker.
8. Add in the broth and the beer. Mix it. Then add in the tomato puree, tomato paste, fire roasted tomatoes, and the polenta to the mix. Stir it well.
9. Add in the beans, ½ tsp. of salt, and the Sucanat. Cook it on high for about 5 hours or on low for 8-9 hours. Stir in the scallion and the cilantro.

Nutritional Information per serving:

Calories: 349 Total Fat: 31g Carb: 31g Protein: 26g

Orange Beef Stew

Ingredients:
- 1 Medium Red Onion – Peeled, Whole
- 8 Whole Cloves
- 1 Pound of Baby Carrots
- 3 Large Sized Parsnips – Peeled, Sliced
- 1 Medium Sweet Onions – Chopped
- 1 ½ Pounds of Chuck Roast – Cut to Cubes
- ¾ tsp. of Salt
- ½ tsp. of Pepper
- 14 Ounces of Stewed Tomatoes – Drained
- 1 Cup of Beef Broth
- 2 Tbsp. of Blackstrap Molasses
- 1 ½ Tbsp. of Apple Cider Vinegar
- 2 Cloves of Garlic – Crushed, Chopped
- 2 tsp. of Orange Zest
- 1 tsp. of Coriander – Ground
- ¼ tsp. of Ground Cinnamon
- 1/3 Cup of Raisins

Directions:
1. Stud your red onion evenly with your cloves. Put it in the cooker.
2. Add in the carrots, sweet onion, and parsnips.
3. Season the cubes of beef with the salt and the pepper. Put it on the top of the vegetables.
4. Pour the tomatoes over the on the beef.
5. In a medium bowl, whisk the broth, vinegar, molasses, garlic, coriander, zest, and the cinnamon. Pour it on the top.
6. Cook it on high for 3-4 hours or for 5-6 hours on high.

7. Add in the raisins during the last 30-minute part of the cooking time.
8. Remove the studded red onion.

Nutritional Information per serving:

Calories: 698 Total Fat: 40g Carb: 54g Protein: 33g

Vegetable Beef

Ingredients:

- 1 Large Sized Sweet Onion – Chopped
- 1 Medium Sized Green Bell Pepper – Seeded, Chopped
- 2 Medium Carrots – Peeled, Sliced
- 2 Parsnips – Peeled, Sliced
- 2 Ribs of Celery – Sliced
- 1 ½ Pound of Stew Beef – Cubed
- 4 Cups of Beef Stock
- 14 ½ Ounces of Tomatoes – Diced Un-drained
- ¼ Cup of Burgundy Wine
- 1 tsp. of Sweet Paprika
- 1 tsp. of Oregano
- 1 tsp. of Basil
- ¾ tsp. of Salt
- ¾ tsp. of Pepper
- 12 Ounces of Green Beans
- ¾ Cup of Pearl Barley

Directions:

1. Combine the bell pepper, onion, carrots, celery, parsnips, and the stew beef in the cooker.
2. Pour the stock and the tomatoes on the top.
3. Add in the paprika, wine, oregano, salt, pepper, and the basil. Cook it on low for 4 hours.
4. Add in the green beans and the barley. Cook it for 2 more hours.

Nutritional Information per serving:

Calories: 396 Total Fat: 5g Carb: 40g Protein: 26g

Dark Cherry Stew

Ingredients:

- 12 Ounces of Dark Cherries – Frozen
- 1 Medium Sized Butternut Squash – Peeled, Seeded, Quartered, Sliced
- 1 Large Sized Sweet Onion – Sliced
- ½ Cup of Juice Sweetened Tart Cherries – Dried
- 1 ¼ Pounds of Stew Meat – Cubed
- 14 Ounces of Tomatoes – Diced, Un-Drained
- 2 Tbsp. of Tapioca – Quick Cooking
- 2 tsp. of Cherry Butter – Un-Sweetened
- ¾ tsp. of Salt
- ½ tsp. of Pepper
- ¼ tsp. of Cinnamon

Directions:

1. Put the frozen cherries, onion, squash, and the dried cherries on the bottom of the cooker.
2. Top it with the beef.
3. In a medium bowl, combine the tapioca, tomatoes, salt, pepper, cherry butter, and the cinnamon. Mix it well.
4. Pour the tomato mix on the top and cook it for 4-5 hours on high or on low for 5-6 hours.

Nutritional Information per serving:

Calories: 253 Total Fat: 5g Carb: 32g Protein: 23g

Jalapeno Beef

- 2 pounds Beef Stew Meat
- 2 cups finely chopped white Onion (1 onion)
- 4 Garlic cloves, minced
- 3/4 cup Beef Broth
- 3 tablespoons Red Curry Paste
- 2 tablespoons Fish Sauce
- 2 tablespoons fresh Lime Juice
- 1 (13.5-ounce) can Coconut Milk
- 2 tbsp. Coconut Oil
- 1 Jalapeño pepper, minced
- Fresh Thai Basil Leaves

Directions:
1. In a skillet, brown beef in coconut oil. Move to slow cooker set on low.
2. Add the red curry paste and fish sauce.
3. Sauté the onions until translucent, add garlic and minced jalapeño. Cook for an additional minute, add to slow-cooker.
4. Add the broth, coconut milk, and lime juice.
5. Cook for at least 6 hours.
6. Serve garnished with Thai basil.

Nutritional Information per serving:

Cal - 492 Carb - 7g, Protein - 48g Fat - 23g

Spicy Shredded Beef Chuck

- 2 pounds Beef Chuck Roast
- 1/2 cup Lime Juice
- 1 tablespoon Tomato Paste
- 1/2 cup Beef Broth
- 1 cup Onion, diced
- 1 Serrano Pepper, diced
- 1 Jalapeno, diced
- 5 cloves Garlic, minced
- 1 tbsp. Red Chili Flakes
- 1 teaspoon Mexican Oregano
- 1 teaspoon Thyme
- Pinch of Nutmeg
- Salt and Pepper to taste

Directions:

1. Add the Beef broth, tomato paste, peppers, seasonings, and lime juice to the slow-cooker on High. Cook at least thirty minutes
2. Add the roast to the slow-cooker, and drop the temp to Low. Cook for 6 to 8 hours.
3. Using two forms, pull apart the meat into shreds. Stir to incorporate all ingredients.

Nutritional Information per serving:

Cal - 350, Carbs - 4g, Protein - 51g, Fat - 12g,

Beef Chuck & Spices

- 4 pound Beef Chuck Roast
- 3-5 medium Carrots, roughly chapped
- 3 stalks Celery, roughly chopped
- 1 medium Onion, cut into chunks
- 3 cloves Garlic, minced
- 1 tbsp. Coconut Flour.
- 3 tablespoons Tomato Paste
- Kosher Salt
- freshly ground Black Pepper
- 3 tablespoons Coconut Oil
- 1 cup and 2 tbsp. Apple Cider Vinegar
- 3 cups Beef Broth
- 3 Bay Leaves
- 1 teaspoon Thyme
- 1 teaspoon Oregano
- 1 teaspoon Rosemary
- 1/2 tea spoon Hot Paprika
- 1/4 teaspoon ground Nutmeg

Directions:

1. Pour oil into a large slow cooker and heat on high for ten minutes.
2. Add thyme, oregano, rosemary, paprika, nutmeg, and garlic to the slow-cooker. Stir and continuing heating for ten more minutes.
3. Add onions, stir to coat with oil/spices, about two minutes. Leave to heat for an hour.
4. Add carrots and celery. Stir for a minute, add the tomato paste, and let cook for an hour.

5. Add broth and 1 cup of vinegar, stir and let heat for 30 minutes.
6. Salt and pepper the roast, then add to the slow-cooker. Let heat on high for ten minutes, then reduce heat to low.
7. Allow to cook for 6 hours minimum, stirring at least every hour.
8. Increase temperature to high for 30 minutes.
9. Remove beef and rest underneath aluminum foil.
10. Mix 2 tbsp to coconut flour, combine, then add to slow-cooker. Allow to cook for at least ten minutes, stirring frequently.

Nutritional Information per serving:

Cal - 357 Carb - 3g Protein - 31g Fat - 14g

Beef Chili

- 2 pounds boneless Beef Sirloin Steak or Top Round Steak, cut into 1/2 inch cubes
- 1 pound Ground Beef
- 1 medium white Onion, chopped
- 2 cloves Garlic, minced
- Avocado Oil
- 2 cups Beef Broth
- 1/2 cup Water
- 1 1/2 tablespoon Chili Powder
- 1 1/2 teaspoon ground Cumin
- 3 teaspoons Mexican Oregano
- 1/2 teaspoon Cayenne Pepper
- 1/2 teaspoon Black Pepper
- Salt
- Chopped fresh Cilantro leaves

1. Using a large skillet, sauté the onion in a tablespoon of Avocado over medium heat, salt, and after they start to look like clouded glass, add the garlic, 1/2 of the chili powder, cumin and oregano, and the black pepper & continue cooking for two minutes.
2. Transfer the mixture to the Slow-cooker on High
3. In the skillet, brown the stew meat in a little avocado oil over medium-high heat.
4. Lightly salt the stew meat, and add to the slow-cooker when completely browned. Stir to combine.
5. In the skillet, brown the ground beef in a little avocado oil. Drain, and add to the slow cooker. Cook for thirty minutes.
6. Add beef broth, water, and remaining spices. Cook for at least two hours, stirring every 30 minutes. .
7. Chop cilantro, adding a bit to the top of each bowl.

Nutritional Information per serving:
Cal - 261, Carb - 4g, Protein - 35g, Fat - 10g,

Oregano Beef Sirloin

- 2 1/2 pounds b\Beef s\Sirloin, cut in to 1/2 inch cubes
- 1 1/2 pounds Tomatillos, husked, cut in half, and rinsed.
- 1 large White Onion, cut into wedges
- 1/4 cup lime juice
- 4 cloves Garlic, minced
- 2 tbsp Mexican Oregano
- Salt
- Black Pepper
- Avocado oil

Directions:
1. Pre-heat oven to 500 degrees.
2. In a large bowl, mix tomatillos, and onion with oil.
3. Arrange Tomatillos and onion on a foil-covered baking tray. Bake for 20 minutes.
4. Allow to cool for 30 minutes.
5. In a skillet, brown the beef, then add to a slow-cooker on high.
6. Add to blender with garlic, lime juice, and 1 tbsp. Oregano. Pulse for 30 seconds. Pour over beef.
7. Cook for at least three hours.

Nutritional Information per serving:

Cal - 243, Carb - 6g, Fat - 7g , Protein - 35g,

Spicy Beef Stew

- 3 pounds Beef Stew Meat
- 2 Habanero Peppers, cut 1/2 through on both sides, but left intact.
- 1 Jalapeno Pepper, de-veined, de-seeded and diced.
- 3 cups Beef Broth
- 1 large Carrot, diced
- 2 Celery Stalks, cut into 1 inch chunks
- 1 large Yellow Onion, cut into chunks
- 3 cloves Garlic
- 3 pieces Galangal
- 1 teaspoon Thyme
- 10 black Peppercorns
- 1 tbsp. Coconut or 1 teaspoon Tapioca Flour
- Olive Oil
- Salt
- White Pepper

1. Into a Slow-cooker on high, add the broth.
2. Add Habaneros to the slow cooker whole with stem intact.
3. In a little olive oil, brown the beef in a skillet over medium-high. Salt, and stir constantly.
4. Using a slotted spoon, remove the beef and add to the slow cooker
5. In the skillet, sauté the onion for a minute over medium heat, then add jalapeño, carrots, and celery and sauté until the onions look like a foggy morning. Add to the slow-cooker.
6. Add galangal, pepper corns, and thyme to the slow-cooker. Cook three to five hours.
7. Remove Galangal and Habaneros.

Nutritional Information per serving:

Cal - 282, Carb. - 3g, Protein - 43g, Fat - 9g,

Garlic Beef Shoulder

- 3 pounds Beef Shoulder, trimmed of the fat
- 10-12 cloves of Garlic, crushed
- 2 cloves of Garlic, sliced thin
- 2 tbsp. Coconut Oil.
- 1 cup Beef Stock
- Sea Salt
- Black Pepper

Directions:

1. Sprinkle the roast with salt and pepper, then place in the fridge for an hour after.
2. Put the coconut oil and sliced garlic into the slow-cooker on high.
3. Remove the meat from the fridge and slather the garlic all over it by hand (it feels REALLY funky!)
4. Place the roast in the slow-cooker, add the stock, lower the temperature to low and leave for at least 8 hours.
5. Remove the beef.
6. The juices can be strained and used to add garlicky goodness to soups or stews.

Nutritional Information per serving:

Cal - 295, Carbs. - 1g, Protein - 35g, Fat - 7g,

Ginger Beef

- 3 pounds Beef Shoulder
- 1-1/2 Tbsp grated Ginger
- 1 teaspoon ground Ginger
- 3 Garlic cloves, minced
- 2 pieces Galangal
- 1 tbsp. Coconut Oil
- 1 cup Vegetable Broth
- Salt
- Black Pepper

Directions:
1. Sprinkle the roast with salt and pepper, then place in the fridge for an hour after.
2. Put the coconut oil, galangal, ground ginger, and 1/2 tbsp. grated ginger into the slow-cooker on high.
3. Remove the meat from the fridge and slather the remaining ginger and the garlic by hand.
4. Place the roast in the slow-cooker, add the stock, lower the temperature to low and leave for at least 8 hours.
5. Remove the beef.
6. The juices can be strained and used to add soups or stews.

Nutritional Information per serving:

Cal - 374, Carb - 1g, Protein - 47g, Fat - 18g,

www.ingramcontent.com/pod-product-compliance
Lightning Source LLC
Chambersburg PA
CBHW071442070526
44578CB00001B/195